RURAL
COMMUNITY
in the
APPALACHIAN
SOUTH

RURAL
COMMUNITY
in the
APPALACHIAN
SOUTH

Patricia Duane Beaver

Appalachian State University

WAVELAND

PRESS, INC.

Prospect Heights, Illinois

For information about this book, write or call:
Waveland Press, Inc.
P.O. Box 400
Prospect Heights, Illinois 60070
(708) 634-0081

Front cover photograph courtesy of the North Carolina Division of Travel and Tourism.

Part of Chapter 6 appeared in different form in *Appalachian Journal* 5(4), © 1978 Appalachian State University, and is reprinted by permission.

Printed in the United States of America

7 6 5 4 3 2

For my husband, Robert White,
and in fond memory of Cratis Williams

CONTENTS

PREFACE 1992

WITH THE beginning of the 1990s, change is a constant in the daily lives of the people and communities described in this book: political turmoil in Europe and the Middle East are of great interest and concern, with the scattered remnants of yellow ribbons reminding them of the many people called up during the 1991 Gulf War; national, state, and local economies are suffering under dwindling resources; small businesses and major industries are closing, some shifting to other regions of the world, leaving unemployment in the wake; increasing awareness of environmental degradation and new insights on the political economy of Appalachia are bringing new attempts to control social change. Many of these same issues translate into tensions which pit old and young, Republicans and Democrats, newcomers and native-born neighbors in ideological struggles about the meaning and form of community.

Significant theoretical developments in the social sciences which have altered the way scholars approach the subject of community have occurred in gender theory (referred to in the text under the heading of sex roles) and political economy, analyzing class differentiation and world system dynamics. While the new insights have not been formally incorporated into this new edition, these subjects and issues are often expressed within the existing descriptions of these communities. Yet there is still another story to be told, the story about the daily lives and ongoing processes of life in rural Appalachia.

In 1973, my quest for a doctorate and a profession in anthropology led me to a small community in Appalachia to conduct doctoral field research. While my origins are in the mountains of western North Carolina, I grew up in the textile mill village of Enka from which my family later moved into the suburbs of Asheville, a moderate-sized city. I felt more suburban than rural in background, and my experiences as a student at Duke University left me more urbane than provincial, I thought. I thus approached rural Appalachia with many of the stereotypes and romantic fantasies about rural mountain life held by any other middle-class consumer of American popular culture of the 1960s and 1970s. I expected the old-timey, quaint — perhaps stalwart — independent farm family in a farm community, familiar with old songs and sustained by older cultural traditions. Instead, I found humans both pleasing and disturbing, few mountain farmers in a rural industrial work force, a complex culture embracing popular music as well as gospel and country music, and a television culture very much part and parcel of wider national and international networks and associations.

I was encouraged to work in the community of Rocky Creek rather than an alternative location in the Little Switzerland resort area where I had initially begun interviews as a caution against focusing on an area that had experienced major change due to tourism. I sought the untouched community of our anthropological imaginations (and perhaps hillbilly stereotypes), to provide the descriptive base on which to measure change in my work. Ironically, my entree into Rocky Creek was my friendship network to Linda and Larry Douthit, themselves newcomers to the mountains.

As my research progressed, several realizations affected the course of my thinking about community. I found the Rocky Creek neighbors' dealings with the Douthits illustrative of significant patterns of neighboring; in the Douthit's resistance to being drawn into neighboring relationships, the importance of those relationships became clear. I saw a then-disturbing pattern of other newcomers — young ex-urbanites — seeking to make a life in rural Appalachia. I was bothered by the disruption of *my* sense of what the traditional Appalachian community should have been: pristine, preserved, isolated, safe from the corruption of urban life. Finally, and also ironically, in trying to gain acceptance into the community, I actually distanced myself at first from these newcomers by claiming my own heretofore ignored mountain heritage. To this end, I sought my own mythic past through conversations with my grandmother

Beaver/Buchanan. Yet I had waited too long; her memory had faded, and she died before I was able to know much of her childhood. Still claiming kinship through the Buchanan family name and history in a town nearby Rocky Creek (that much I knew for certain), I laid claim to shared ethnicity with the "real" residents of Rocky Creek.

My research in Appalachia led me to Appalachian State University in 1974, so that I could complete my study of Appalachia; I realized that I had only touched the surface. My husband and I moved to Boone, North Carolina and rented a house in a rural community, partly because we found it agreeable, partly to stay in touch with rural communities. Here in Watauga County, I gathered data which confirmed and clarified patterns I was describing in my dissertation on Rocky Creek. Three years later, we bought an old farmstead in yet another community, and began to conduct interviews in Ashe county, as well as to participate in the life of the community in which we lived as neighbors and land-owners. Combining teaching, research, and writing, I completed my dissertation on the Rocky Creek community in 1976.

In 1978 I was named the director of the newly organized Center for Appalachian Studies at Appalachian State University. In my emerging role as advocate for the study of Appalachia, I became aware of the awkward relationship between academia and the surrounding area. The town-gown split commonly associated with universities was aggravated by the town-gown-hillbilly tension. I also became involved in a major study of landownership in Appalachia, which convinced me not only of the extent of outside control on local land and thus the political economy of Appalachia, but also of the importance of participatory research — citizen involvement not only in decision making and planning, but also in research which affects them. I also began to understand the importance of both accountability to the people whom one describes in ethnography, and of making my work accessible to those about whom I write. There is much in the popular media focused on the quaint and the old-timey, buttressing the "hillbilly" image, while disregarding the reality of daily life. In the search for sustaining traditions, celebration of the old has often ignored the new, as mobile homes have replaced log cabins and shift work and weekend farming replaced the small farm economy. Finally, in seeking an alternative to the community study approach to ethnography (since the issues that concerned me transcended the bounds of Rocky Creek), I chose to discuss community as process. However, missing from my own writing was the texture, the color, the humanity, the story of rural people in Appalachia.

Myriad new developments in narrative ethnography were instructive and liberating for me. Here was the story, freed from constraints which often confine ethnography to scholars and their students. But writing narrative was a skill in which I had not trained. I thus sought help in an Appalachian Writers's Workshop at Hindman, Kentucky, under the guidance of writers including James Still, Harriet Arnow, Jim Wayne Miller, and Gurney Norman, all of whom captured the story in Appalachia through fiction or poetry and whose work I have used as enthography in my teaching. At Hindman, I developed the first part of a first chapter of this book, a passage on the flood of November 1977 (chapter 2). (I never actually had the courage to seek the advice of these writers, despite their friendship; I hoped that their skills would seep into my text through association.)

The flood was an important symbol for the process of activating community ties which are otherwise in little evidence. I witnessed that flood from my own porch, and had wandered about the community with my husband and our neighbors surveying the damage.

Because of my work as an administrator and teacher, I had little time to spare, and my writing proceeded slowly. Each season that passed saw my family more engaged in the life of communities like those about which I sought to write. I had laid claim to an Appalachian heritage with which I began to come to terms. I was both of the culture and very distant from it. I saw, through the experiences of my students and the growing literature on ethnicity, that biculturalism was indeed part and parcel of my own experience. I learned that my ambivalence was neither unique to me nor to rural Appalachia.

Out-migration to urban centers and industrial labor is an important part of mountain life that deserves the attention of scholars. In addition, the Appalachian Land Ownership Study confirmed the paucity of small farm ownership throughout rural Appalachia; the image of Appalachia as the land of the small farmer was truly inappropriate and out of date. My own family's experiences over the course of four generations, in moving away from the farm and into the industrial work force fit into a common pattern. Gradually, in my writing my own heritage began to creep into the text.

Despite my claim to ethnicity, my closest rural friends were back-to-the-landers, newcomers who shared both a desire to live in the pleasant surroundings afforded in the mountains, and an urban, liberal, ecologically oriented approach, which many refer to as the mountain counterculture. The back-to-the-land movement was a significant force to be reckoned with, as was the movement of "Florida people" (second-home residents in mountain dwellings), and I began to describe the role of these outsiders/newcomers in rural communities in a chapter subsequently called "Foreigners." Because I was a newcomer, my experience of moving in, gaining acceptance, receiving the benefits, and bearing the pressures of neighboring provided a basis upon which to build a perspective about others' experiences as newcomers. My friends, students, and I had experienced the same phenomenon, so I called upon my own social network for evaluation and critique of my descriptions and conclusions about the back-to-the-land chapter.

As an educator teaching primarily undergraduate students, I engage my students both in their own research and in review of my writing. With the establishment of the masters degree program in Appalachian Studies, I used my graduate students as a sounding board for evaluation of my work, as well. My native-born students provided valuable insights and criticism, and through their commentary, they too began entering the text. The commentary of Mary Greene and Mary Jane Putzel were particularly insightful in helping me clarify my own understanding of gender, family, and landownership. In their explanations to me, their own stories entered the text.

My pregnancy in 1980 and the birth of my first child brought forth commentary from neighbors and regional students that I never would have seen had I not been the object of discussion and advice. The predictions about its sex, warnings about marking the child, experiences with and stories from the hospital staff, and visits from neighbors and relatives were patterns both observed and lived.

In a visit to Rocky Creek, I learned that my wedding at my parents' home, described in an article in the Asheville newspaper which was read and circulated in Rocky Creek, had been emulated by a Rocky Creek friend; his departure from the common pattern of elopement or the newer pattern of the church wedding was remarkable. In addition, my dissertation included matter-of-fact statements about the prevalence of elopement, yet missing were the passion and pain and intrigue which I had not appreciated. Then, awakened early one morning by my neighbor's futile search for her own eloped daughter, and shocked by her unfounded accusations of my collusion, I realized a new dimension to a parent's suffering, and gradually came to understand the acceptance which follows. I was compelled to write more carefully about the phenomenon that I had treated lightly and dispassionately, and probably had not clearly understood.

Likewise, I had written about violence among kin as historical fact. The lived agony surrounding the death of a man at the hands of his own kinsman, and the daily grief which complicates community relationships following the reacceptance of the perpetrator into his community are often only dimly reflected in abstractions. I have not succeeded in capturing this story; the suffering and high feelings which I saw in the life of the widow and surviving children, and the relationships among neighbors in the passing years, remain too sensitive to permit public discourse, and the description which remains, lifted wholecloth from my dissertation, is rather lifeless. I am not yet able to fully explore some issues because scrutinizing them can do harm to the survivors.

Incorporating a narrative style resulted from my experiences of living in the communities about which I wrote and advocacy of the people who are the subject of my inquiry. I hope to make my research accessible to those who are the subject of inquiry, to the scholarly community, and to students whom I teach about culture. While few of my students are from the mountain region, many are from rural places from which they come to college to escape; they have learned to look with disdain upon rural life and the constraints of family obligations, and at times are intellectually awakened by recognizing kinship with people and patterns in the text. In the lives of these people in rural Appalachia, they may glimpse aspects of their own lives, and hence, more fully grasp the meaning and personal struggle of change. Yet close involvement in one's subject has its drawbacks in the moral decisions which must be made with regard to accountability: I am fully accountable and thus must be absolutely honest; I am fully accountable and must therefore obscure data in seeking truth.

Having chosen to incorporate narrative ethnography into the telling of a part of an Appalachian story, I have struggled to hear more clearly, to use the language more precisely and passionately, to communicate the human story with more truth. The struggle has been difficult, satisfying, and a challenge which has affected my writing about Appalachia, the American South, and my newer research relating to Chinese gender, family, and community.

Many colleagues have contributed to my understanding of and approach to Appalachia, through their collaboration, instruction, example in advocacy, scholarship, encouragement, and conversations. I owe particular tribute to Cratis Williams, Helen Lewis, John Gaventa, Rich Humphrey, Carol Stack, John Stephenson, Carole Hill, Jim Wayne Miller, Jerry Williamson, Maggie McFadden, Ron Eller, Gurney Norman, Gregory Reck, Susan Keefe, Jeff Boyer, Steve Fisher, Burt Purrington, Loyal Jones, Ray Moretz, David Whisnant, Judy Cornett, Ann Ritchie, Mary Greene, Mary Jane Putzel, Eric Olsen. My parents, Katherine and Charles Beaver, have been a constant source of encouragement and support. My husband, Robert White, has worked side-by-side with me from the very first visit to Rocky Creek to this day. His observations of the male point of view enhance my understanding, and his critical insights are central to this work. While reading every page (and typing a few), he has sustained, critiqued, and supported my work and our life together in rural Appalachia and China, and I am deeply grateful.

Patricia D. Beaver
Boone, NC
January, 1992

UPDATED RECOMMENDED REFERENCES

Batteau, Allen. 1991. *The Invention of Appalachia*. Tucson: University of Arizona Press.

Dorgan, Howard. 1989. *The Old Regular Baptists of Central Appalachia: Brothers and Sisters in Hope*. Knoxville: University of Tennessee Press.

_____. 1987. *Giving Glory to God in Appalachia: Worship practices of six Baptist subdenominations*. Knoxville: University of Tennessee Press.

Ergood, Bruce and Bruce E. Kuhre. eds. 1991. *Appalachia: Social Context Past and Present*. Dubuque, IA: Kendall/Hunt Publishing Company.

Foster, Stephen. 1988. *The Past is Another Country*. Berkeley and Los Angeles: University of California Press.

Gaventa, John, Barbara Ellen Smith, and Alex Willingham. eds. 1990. *Communities in Economic Crisis: Appalachian and the South*. Philadelphia: Temple University Press.

Halperin, Rhoda H. 1990. *The Livelihood of Kin: Making Ends Meet "The Kentucky Way."* Austin: University of Texas Press.

Keefe, Susan E. 1988. *Appalachian Mental Health*. Lexington: University of Kentucky Press.

Lewis, Helen, et.al. eds. *Picking up the Pieces: Women in and out of work in the rural south*. New Market, TN: Highlander Research and Education Center.

Lewis, Helen and Suzanna O'Donnell, eds. 1990. Ivanhoe History Book — Vol. I, *Remembering Our Past, Building Our Future*. Ivanhoe, VA: Ivanhoe Civic League.

_____. 1990. Ivanhoe History Book — Vol. II, *Telling Our Stories, Sharing Our Lives*. Ivanhoe, VA: Ivanhoe Civic League.

Montel, William L. 1986. *Killings: Folk Justice in the Upper South*. Lexington: University Press of Kentucky.

Titon, Jeff Todd. 1988. *Powerhouse for God. Speech, Chant, and Song in an Appalachian Baptist Church*. Austin: University of Texas Press.

Turner, William H. 1985. *Blacks in Appalachia*. Lexington: University Press of Kentucky.

Van Willigan, John. 1989. *Gettin' Some Age on Me: Social Organization of Older People in a Rural American Community*. Lexington: University Press of Kentucky.

Waller, Altina. 1988. *Feud: Hatfields, McCoys, and social change in Appalachia, 1860-1900*. Chapel Hill: University of North Carolina Press.

RECOMMENDED FILMS

From Appalshop Film, Inc., Box 743, 306 Madison St., Whitesburg, KY 41858:

> In the Good Old Fashioned Way (1973)
> Nature's Way (1973)
> Quilting Women (1976)
> Waterground (1977)
> The Big Lever — Party Politics in Leslie County, Kentucky (1982)
> Coalmining Women (1982)
> Lord and Father (1983)
> Strangers & Kin: A History of the Hillbilly Image (1984)
> Sunny Side of Life (1985)
> Long Journey Home (1987)
> On Our Own Land (1988)
> Chemical Valley (1991)

Other titles from Appalshop deal with Appalachian folk culture, music, traditional arts, coal mining, social change.

For information on film/video titles prior to 1984 see Laura Schuster and Sharyn McCrumb. 1984. "Appalachian Film List." *Appalachian Journal* 11(4):329-383.

For information on feature films see "The Hills Meet Hollywood: The *Now and Then* Guide to Selected Feature Films about Appalachia." *Now and Then*, Fall 1991, 8(3): 8-12.

INTRODUCTION

THIS BOOK describes several aspects of the social organization and system of values of the rural community in the
southern Appalachian Mountains, specifically in western
North Carolina. Research was conducted over a ten-year
period beginning in 1973 in three rural communities in three
western North Carolina counties. Research conducted in
1973 and 1974 is described in my doctoral dissertation,
"Symbols and Social Organization in an Appalachian Mountain Community" (1976), and focuses on the community that
I call Rocky Creek. Subsequent research was conducted in
two other communities, which I call Plum Tree and Grassy
Fork. I have used pseudonyms for these three communities
and for all of the people mentioned in this analysis.

Rather than describing a single community, this discussion considers community itself, a combination of elements
linking geographically defined place, the daily lives and relationships of people, historical experiences, and shared
values.[1] Drawing from a data base of three separate and, of
course, unique communities, I have focused my analysis on
social patterns and cultural systems common to these three
places and to similar southern Appalachian rural communities. Thus a specific narrative, set in one place, may com-
prise elements and references from two or even three of the
communities. For example, chapter 2 begins with events
surrounding the November 1977 flooding, the impact of
which was felt throughout southern Appalachia. While the
narrative unfolds through the viewpoint of one family as it
interacts with its neighbors and kin, similar exchanges were

taking place in rural communities throughout the area. Thus the major themes of this work are concerned with patterns and values that crosscut specific locales.

The mountain community in rural western North Carolina has been shaped by the adaptation of ethnically diverse family groups to the resource base and the terrain. The nineteenth century saw the growth of largely self-sufficient agricultural communities. Following the destruction caused by the Civil War, the decision to exploit the region's timber resources prompted completion of a rail system in western North Carolina and marked the beginning of major changes in social relations, land ownership, land use, and the regional economy. Rail lines not only facilitated the development of the timber industry but also led the way for tourism and recreation industries and consequent immigration, out-migration, and growth of a variety of other industries.

This description of community focuses on the organization of kin, friends, enemies, and neighbors into networks of association and on the organization of values that bind people into community. Persisting through dramatic social and economic changes in rural Appalachia in the past decades, community is a moral system in which participants offer mutual aid; it comes into poignant focus in times of communitywide crisis.

While neighbors share moral or ideological bonds, specific social ties, based primarily on kinship, give form and substance to community. Kin ties provide potential networks of association, specific links that people can call upon when the need arises.[2] Kinship also provides an idiom for the way in which people should behave toward one another and is one of several bases, including friendship, residential proximity, and economic obligations, for the formation of groups. Kin ties connect community residents into a system giving personal identity through the expression of common roots, shared experiences, and shared values. Kinship is thus more than simple genealogical relationship; it is a cultural idea through which relationships are expressed and from which community homogeneity is derived.[3]

As kin ties give form and substance to community, sex

roles define appropriate behavior for social adults. Gender-defined relations of power and influence, both within the family and within the community, shift as the individual moves through the life cycle and likewise are affected by a changing economy. The movement of women into the labor force, particularly since the 1950s, has resulted in a variety of changes in the relative status of women in the public sector, as compared with their status in the traditional community context.

The population of the rural southern Appalachian community has not been static; particularly since the 1960s, increasing numbers of nonlocal people have begun to live in rural mountain communities. Besides summer tourists and retirees, a new group—back-to-the-landers—has begun to shape, and to be shaped by, community networks and processes. The increasing population of back-to-the-landers in the mountains has resulted in the formation of new types of ties, both for the traditional community and for the immigrants.

Pervading the ideology of community are two important values: independence and egalitarianism. Both values are viewed as myths; history provides the "mythic charter" of the community, since history may be interpreted to justify existing beliefs. Community homogeneity is expressed in terms of the collective representation of the community's own historical mythic charter, involving the notions of common ancestry, shared experience, kinship, and rootedness in place. Cooperation among residents is achieved through mutual aid, and egalitarianism, despite obvious socioeconomic differences, is idealized and reinforced through various leveling mechanisms.

I conducted my research primarily in three communities.

ROCKY CREEK

With a population of approximately 185, Rocky Creek lies in the southern Appalachian mountain region of western North Carolina. Like most rural Appalachian communities, Rocky Creek is clearly defined geographically, bounded on the north, south, east, and west by series of mountain ridges reaching elevations of roughly 3,800, 3,600, 2,800, and 4,000 feet. The community exists in the hollow lying between these ridges. Big and Little Rocky Creeks course their ways through the community, flowing down the northern slopes and joining at the northwestern, or lower end, of the community before flowing into the Toe River. Rocky Creek is considered part of the Toe River Valley, an important feature in the settlement and politics of the area; the river itself defines part of the county line.

Rocky Creek is in Yancey County, the county seat of which is Burnsville, a town of about 1,400 located approximately seven miles, or twenty minutes' driving time, from the community. Most residents travel often to Burnsville for groceries, farm supplies, and other shopping or business in the various retail stores located there. The county offices, supermarkets, farm supply companies, hardware stores, clothing and general merchandise stores, restaurants, movie theater, factories, motel, hotel, and consolidated county schools are located in or near Burnsville, so Rocky Creek residents find many reasons to travel to town, often on a daily basis.

Each summer Burnsville sees the influx of a large number of tourists and summer people, an increasing number of whom have built or purchased second homes in Rocky Creek. Many are attracted to the area not only by the scenic beauty of this county with the highest average elevation in the state (with five of the highest peaks east of the Mississippi, including the highest, Mount Mitchell) but also by a variety of unique cultural attractions, including a summer theater workshop organized by the University of North Carolina at Greensboro and, through the cooperative efforts of residents of the immigrant artist community and native-born supporters, performances by visiting classical musicians sponsored by the local arts organization. Instruction in traditional and modern crafts draws visitors to Penland School of Crafts. Rocky Creek residents sometimes join summer tourists in attending summer crafts fairs as exhibitors and spectators.

Rocky Creek, like Plum Tree and Grassy Fork, can be reached only by private transportation. There is no public transportation in the county; the train that passed close to the community several times a week as late as the mid-1970s stopped carrying passengers long ago and has now ceased operation altogether.

The houses in Rocky Creek, most of which adjoin the road, are predominantly one-story wood frame, usually clapboard painted white or stuccoed; some sport new aluminum siding. Two old, hand-hewn log cabins remain, remnants of a past century. Several log barns remain standing as well, although their days of functional use are past. Newer barns of sawed lumber have gradually replaced the old. A few two-story frame houses, built around the turn of the century, also occur, as well as a fair number of newer brick homes, including several ranch style. Newest of all are the mobile homes, increasing in number yearly. Finally, a gradually increasing number of second homes are tucked into newly cleared and bulldozed house sites high above the valley floor and the main road.

The community school closed years ago, and no traces remain of the building; the store and post office, once located at the mouth of the hollow, likewise closed long ago. A family-owned general merchandise store, located less than a mile from the entrance to the communty, is a frequent gathering place where people can buy a gallon of milk, a loaf of bread, or five gallons of gas. Two churches, one Baptist and one Methodist, are found at opposite ends of the community; besides the two cemeteries located behind these churches, four other family cemeteries can be found on high hillsides overlooking the community.

PLUM TREE

Located approximately forty miles from Rocky Creek and about seven miles from Boone in Watauga County, the Plum Tree community has a population of approximately 350 people living in just over 100 households. Like Rocky Creek, Plum Tree's settlement, history, and community growth were shaped by the lay of the land and by the courses of Plum Tree Creek and Jones Creek, which join before emptying into the

New River. The creeks drain the higher ridges, which reach approximately 4,000 and 5,500 feet in elevation and form the community's perimeters. One primary road through Plum Tree follows the course of Plum Tree Creek, while various secondary gravel roads lead to a number of dwellings located up the hillsides from the main valley floor.

Four churches, two Baptist, one Methodist, and one Assembly of God, are located along the main Plum Tree road, although, as in Rocky Creek, many residents attend churches outside the community. The last remnants of the first church in the community, the Lutheran church, were removed during the late 1970s. Two family-owned and family-operated general stores and gas stations are located in Plum Tree, and a volunteer fire department serves the community as well as the surrounding area. The elementary school is located a few miles from the community; older students attend the county's one consolidated high school in Boone.

Two locally owned sawmills and a small manufacturing company each employ a small number of residents, although most families are supported by the labor of members who travel daily to work for a variety of employers in and around Boone, in the resort developments beyond Boone, or in industries in Lenoir. With a resident population of about ten thousand, Boone is the county seat of Watauga County; Appalachian State University is located in Boone, with a student population of over ten thousand. The population swells each year with summer residents and tourists and with seasonal visitors to local ski resorts. Boone has a wide variety of businesses, industries, recreational facilities, and services that benefit the Plum Tree community.

After a period of population decline, characteristic of most rural Appalachian mountain communities during the 1950s and 1960s, Plum Tree has experienced marked population growth during the 1970s and early 1980s as the urban population of Watauga County has expanded dramatically and new residents are seeking a home in a rural community. Rather than large acreage, newcomers are seeking a modest amount of land—enough for a garden spot and the opportunity for rural living.

GRASSY FORK

About fifteen miles from Plum Tree, the Grassy Fork community lies in Ashe County. Grassy Fork has a resident population of approximately 240 in about 75 households, while another 5 families occupy second homes in the community on a seasonal basis. Three churches, one Methodist and two Baptist, are located in the community; the two Grassy Fork stores, the post office, and the school closed years ago, but a family-owned general merchandise store and a gas station are located nearby. Public school students travel approximately forty-five minutes to the rural elementary school located downriver on the New River or an hour to one of the three consolidated county high schools.

West Jefferson, the county seat, is located about twenty miles away, and some residents travel to work in various jobs and industries in and around West Jefferson or Jefferson. Yet, a number of Grassy Fork residents also travel to Boone, about a twenty-five-mile drive, because of the variety of jobs available in the university, the hospital, or the various retail stores and industries. Other residents have found work over the state line in Johnson County, Tennessee, in a town of 2,100 that is located approximately twenty minutes away by car.

As in Rocky Creek and Plum Tree, community development and community boundaries were shaped by the terrain and by the possibilities of farming the valleys drained by Grassy Creek, a tributary of the New River.

Chapter One

THE COMMUNITIES IN CONTEXT

THE APPALACHIAN mountain area is composed of three parallel belts running roughly northeast to southwest.[1] On the east, the Blue Ridge Mountains form the first belt, rising from the eastern Piedmont, with the highest peaks in the Great Smoky and Black mountains. The Blue Ridge Belt, a narrow ten to sixteen miles wide in Maryland and Virginia, widens to a maximum of seventy miles, forming a high plateau in North Carolina, with Mount Mitchell as its highest peak at an elevation of 6,684 feet. It gradually diminishes in height to the south, merging into the Piedmont Plateau in Georgia. The average altitude ranges from over 3,000 feet to almost 6,000 feet in North Carolina. While the eastern slopes of the Blue Ridge are rugged with rivers and streams cascading through deep gorges, the western side slopes more gradually, as broad valleys are watered by gently descending steams until they create narrow cuts in the northwest edge of the plateau.

To the west of the Blue Ridge lies the second belt, the Great Valley, or Appalachian Valley; this valley provided a major European migration and settlement route to the entire southern United States, as well as into the eastern Piedmont and the mountains. An extension of the Cumberland Valley in Pennsylvania, it becomes the Shenandoah Valley, or the Valley of Virginia, as it moves south. More accurately considered valley and ridge, the valley belt as a whole is upland; from an altitude of 500 feet at Harper's Ferry, West Virginia, it reaches 2,600 to 2,700 feet in southwest Virginia before tapering off to 550 feet or less in Alabama.

West of the Appalachian Valley, the third belt—the Allegheny-Cumberland Plateau—rises as a wall on its eastern side and gradually slopes down on its northwestern side, reaching heights of 4,000 feet in Virginia and Kentucky before tapering down to about 3,000 feet in Tennessee. All of West Virginia, eastern Kentucky, and eastern Tennessee lie within the plateau belt, which extends into northern Alabama before sloping off to the south. The plateau has been dissected and carved by elaborate stream networks; in this region are found some of the richest coal seams in the United States.

The native vegetation of the area was predominantly mixed deciduous forest including a variety of oak, hickory, maple, tulip poplar, walnut, and chestnut. Pine and hemlock communities were found in special edaphic and topographic settings and in early succession forests. Black spruce and fraser fir clusters characterize the highest elevations. "Barrens," or prairie pockets, were scattered over the region, possibly as a result of Indian firedrives. Dominant game animals included white-tailed deer, elk, black bear, turkey, and passenger pigeons.

Prior to European settlement the Cherokee Indians were dominant in the southern and central Appalachians. While much of their territory was hunting ground, the Cherokee population was concentrated in villages along riverbanks in eastern Tennessee, western North Carolina, northern Georgia, and northwestern South Carolina. The Cherokees probably had been residents in the area for at least four thousand years, exploiting the variety of ecological niches available in the southern Appalachian environment. Spanish expeditions led by de Soto in 1540 and Juan Pardo in 1567 first brought Europeans into the mountains in search of gold. Fur traders established permanent outposts as early as 1650. As European settlers followed fur traders down the valleys and into the mountains and established permanent homesteads, contact took an increasing toll on the Cherokee population through disease and warfare, drastically reducing their numbers and their access to traditional hunting lands.

Following the devastation of the Cherokees by first the British and later the Americans in the American Revolution,

American Indian policy stressed "pacification" of the Cherokees and "inaugurated a program to 'civilize' the 'savages' through the introduction of white farming techniques" (Perdue 1979). The cumulative effects of disease, disruption of traditional subsistence-economy systems, loss of territory, Indian slave trade, and conflicts with whites likewise forced the Cherokees to "reevaluate their traditional ways and to develop a system that would stand up to these new challenges" (French and Hornbuckle 1981:16). A period of cultural, political, and economic revolution followed, including the development of plantations and a capitalist economy in certain Cherokee areas in the southern Appalachians, before the disruption of the eastern Cherokees with the removal of 1838.

By the late eighteenth century, the European population of the southern Appalachians had begun to increase dramatically, fed primarily by successive waves of Scotch-Irish and German immigrants increasing about 1717 and reaching a peak in midcentury. Beginning in 1717 and ending in 1775, the Scotch-Irish left northern Ireland in five waves of migration because of economic restrictions from England that crippled the prosperous wool and linen industries and because of rack-renting, drought and famine, and religious oppression (Ford 1966; Leyburn 1962). German immigration was likewise motivated by economic and political oppression and by mounting tax burdens on propertied classes.

ROCKY CREEK

Settlement of western North Carolina was well under way by the late eighteenth and early nineteenth centuries. The first family of white settlers in Rocky Creek apparently moved in by 1790 (although one woman believed her family to have arrived in 1750). Early settlement patterns in the area followed the course of the Toe River, the larger river into which Big and Little Rocky Creeks empty; families settled in the Rocky Creek hollow and in other such hollows where streams flowed into the river from the surrounding mountain ridges. There were eighty families, or three hundred people, inhabiting the Toe River Valley by 1790 (Deyton 1947:434). The Colonial Act of 1778 first officially opened the western North Carolina mountains to white settlers, although set tlers were already well established prior to that time. Hundreds of land grants for hundreds and thousands of acres of land were taken out by speculators in minerals, timber, and land. Thus the colonization of the mountains, a process of exploitation described by Lewis and Knipe (1970), had begun well before settlement was even well under way.

A multitide of uncertainties surround any investigation of the specific origins of early settlers in particular mountain communities. The Scotch-Irish and Germans, predominant in the early settlement, were joined by English, French, Swiss, Welsh, Dutch, Scots, other Europeans, and Africans. The first Rocky Creek settler apparently was the son of a Tory who came from eastern North Carolina to escape persecution for his father's activities. At least one settler in the Toe River valley area seems to have come from London as an indentured servant and had worked in Boston before making his way south (Shepperd 1935:20-21). Several families came from Tennessee settlements; others identify Scotch-Irish ancestry, with the point of entry having been either Pennsylvania or South Carolina (Charleston). Several families thought their ancestors were Germans who had migrated from settlements in Virginia, while several others suggested origins in piedmont North Carolina.

Early Rocky Creek was typically rich with abundant game, fish, water, land, and other forest resources. Early inhabitants, after clearing land and homesteading, were dependent on subsistence farming and on cooperation with the few neighbors, supplemented by hunting, fishing, and the gathering of forest products. Throughout the southern Appalachians, isolated homesteads were uncommon, even during the settlement period, since settlers came in the company of other families and located near each other for assistance, protection, and community (Eller 1982; Wilhelm 1978). While settlement was often dispersed, particularly in a linear fashion, as settlers followed each other up the hollows, homesteads were not isolated from each other.

One problem for early agriculture and livestock raising that was recorded in the Rocky Creek area was "varmints." Panthers, wolves, wildcats, and bears sometimes preyed on domesticated stock that were allowed to run free, and they disrupted attempts at gardening. From 1836 to 1852 a wolf tax was levied, the proceeds of which supplied a bounty for wolf scalps (Deyton 1947:438). As late as the 1930s, residents recalled "snaking the beds" and taking other precautions against varmints (Shepperd 1935). Settlement and subsistence depended upon clearing the land of virgin forests to make way for log houses and outbuildings, garden spots, and grazing land. With increasing population density and land clearing, the amount of food available from wild game diminished, so that hunting eventually became relegated to the very important realm of sport.

Such nonindigenous but important items as salt, sugar, coffee, baking soda, and medicines were obtained from market centers in Georgia and South Carolina. Because of the poor conditions of roads, transportation of goods to market, and of supplies back, was extremely difficult. The lack of easy access to market centers to the east and south required Rocky Creek families to be self-sufficient. Sugar from sources other than cane was produced and later marketed in the form of maple sugar and syrup from sugar maple trees, molasses from cultivated sorghum, and honey.

In 1840 the population of Yancey County, in which Rocky Creek is located, was 5,500. While subsistence farming was the predominant economic activity, the variety of other institutions in the county included thirty-two distilleries, forty-three gristmills, three sawmills, and two ironworks. Four people were recorded as manufacturing hats, caps, and bonnets, and one man tanned leather. Dairy products for that year were valued at $5,000, followed by orchard products at $4,000 and homemade or family-produced goods at $4,500. No one in the county earned income from garden products for market or from retail trade, since there was no access to markets. Yet, one forest product exploited by 1840, for which there were local buyers, was ginseng; others were medicinal herbs such as bloodroot, witch hazel, raspberry leaves, spearmint, and liverwort (Deyton 1947:454). Such forest products were valued at $5,500.

Liquor was produced from surplus grain crops and orchard produce, primarily for local consumption (Deyton 1947:458) but also as a means of converting surplus crops into cash in outland markets. A bushel of shelled corn could be converted into liquor and transported to market more easily than whole corn. In 1840 the thirty-two recorded distilleries in the county produced 5,900 gallons of distilled and fermented liquors, serving an important economic and social function in the region:

> The distilling, retailing, and drinking of spiritous liquors were common among all classes. Even ministers in many instances are said to have made and sold whiskey. It was considered right to convert the surplus corn, rye, and fruits into whiskey and brandy, some of which was probably exported. The statement is attributed to [the Civil War sheriff] of Yancey County that he sold 1,200 gallons of whiskey in Shelby, Charlotte, and South Carolina towns in 1859, and that the proceeds enabled him to discharge his share of the bond of a former sheriff who had absconded. . . . [However,] local demand required the greater part of the amount distilled. . . . Drinking was prevalent on all public occasions. . . . It seems that there was little or no objection to whiskey on religious grounds during the period. [Deyton 1947:457-58]

By 1860 the population of the county had passed eight thousand, of which 375 persons were slaves. There were thirty-one manufacturing concerns in the county, of which two dealt in blacksmithing, eighteen in flour and meal, two in leather, seven in sawed lumber, and two in wool carding. These thirty-one concerns employed a total of thirty-five people and together produced $50,000 worth of goods.

The early trend in agriculture was diversification, with a concentration on livestock production. Of the 312,000 acres of farmland in the county, 46,000 acres had been timbered (listed as improved) for farming purposes by 1860. Livestock production was well under way, and stock was valued at $333,000. Grains and cereals, led by corn (with 245,000 bushels harvested), were important farm crops; hay, wheat, rye, and oats all figured in the diversification that subsistence required. The value of market garden products was $12,000 by this time. Orchard products, particularly apples, were also important and had a value of $21,000. Also significant were maple sugar (4,800 pounds), sorghum molasses (22,000 gallons), and honey (28,000 pounds). The value of homemade manufactures exceeded $43,000. Although 17,000 pounds of tobacco were produced in the county in 1860, tobacco did not become particularly important to the local or regional economy until after the introductin of burley tobacco to the mountains in 1923 (Van Noppen and Van Noppen 1973:277).

Because of the difficulty of transportation, the sale value of goods produced in the mountains before the coming of the railroad and improved roads in the twentieth century was difficult to realize. Some livestock was sold to drovers from Kentucky and Tennessee, who drove hogs, cattle, and mules through the valley area and on to markets in the Atlantic seaboard: "The marketing of stock was not always certain, but in many instances owners were able to sell to drovers who were passing through the county. Otherwise, local buyers and sometimes the owners themselves would drive the stock to the cotton belt or even to Charleston and dispose of the animals at low prices" (Deyton 1947:451) With regard to the difficult problem of converting local surpluses into either cash or nonindigenous items, "It was the custom for several families to pool such articles as they possessed for export, such as bacon, lard, dried fruit, deer hams, honey, and beeswax, and to have these carried to market. From thirty to sixty days were required for the round trip, and the cost of one-way transportation ranged from $1.75 to $2.00 per hundredweight, thus consuming a large portion of the receipts" (Deyton 1947:453).

It has been estimated that there are up to one hundred kinds of trees in western North Carolina, and well into the twentieth century, the area was a lumberman's paradise. Yet, prior to the coming of the railroad, a large part of the cleared timber that was not used for log structures, household furnishings, farming equipment, or fuel was allowed to rot or was burned off:

> Although the forest was thought of as an obstacle to home building, it was the chief resource of the people. In a small way the early settlers were all lumbermen. Their principal tool was the axe, with which they marked their trails and chopped the trees for logs to build their cabins and for fuel. They girdled, cut, and burned the trees they wanted to get rid of. They were as apt to build their rail fences of choice black walnut as of pine or oak if the walnut was handier. They burned the woodlands so their livestock would have better pasturage. [Van Noppen and Van Noppen 1973:291-92]

As with every other economic asset in the region, the major difficulty with marketing lumber was transportation of the goods to market centers. Some timber was dragged out with ox teams, "six and eight head to a wagon, but they couldn't haul much even then, not with an axle draggin' in the mud. Those days were hard on everybody—oxen and mules and folks" (Shepperd 1935:59). Because of marketing difficulties, only a small percentage of the marketable lumber ever reached the markets. A great deal of lumber went into farm buildings, fences, and fuel.

PLUM TREE

In Watauga County, only 40 miles away from Rocky Creek as the crow flies but a good two hours' drive by car, lies the Plum Tree community, whose early settlement history closely parallels that of Rocky Creek. While first a hunting camp, which Daniel Boone and other less well known personages are reported to have occupied, the community saw its first permanent settlers in the early 1800s. Settlers in Plum Tree followed the course of the New River in order to reach the Plum Tree Creek tributary. Beginning first on the lower reaches of Plum Tree Creek, settlement slowly spread up the hollow.

In the mid-1830s, a group of German families who had been living in piedmont North Carolina moved into the Plum Tree area, bringing with them not only agricultural skills but a variety of other skills useful on the frontier (as carpenters, millwrights, and stonemasons) and a determination to continue their Lutheran heritage (Moretz n.d.). The organizer of this major move of families into Plum Tree, John Moretz, bought an existing gristmill, which he rebuilt; "in addition to being the miller, a farmer, carpenter, and the postmaster, John Moretz helped organize a Lutheran congregation and served as one of the first elders after the church was formally organized in 1845" (Moretz n.d.:8).

Mountain farms during the preindustrial period in southern Appalachia were family-based units and included a mixture of bottomland and hillside or mountainside. One young man who moved to Plum Tree with the group of German families married the daughter of another German immigrant, whereupon they moved farther up Plum Tree Creek, bought a tract of land, and built a two-story log home. They later built a mill for grinding their own and their neighbors' corn and other grains. The husband was a miller, "farmer, blacksmith, wheelwright, and worked in timbering," and his wife "operated a spinning wheel and a loom and had a major role in raising and providing for a large family of 13 children" (Moretz n.d.:8).

As above-average landowners, this family grew, gathered, or constructed almost everything they needed from their farm. They also "traded within and outside the community." Their livestock inventory for 1860 included "3 horses, 2 working oxen, 3 milk cows and 3 other cattle, 26 sheep, and 20 swine." While some animals were slaughtered for food, "three milk cows produced 100 pounds of butter during the year and the sheep provided 50 pounds of wool." In addition, "the farm produced 20 bushels of rye, 24 bushels of buckwheat, 100 bushels of corn, 50 bushels of oats," and a small amount of wheat. "Gardens provided 10 bushels of peas and beans, 25 bushels of Irish potatoes, and a variety of other produce which was canned and preserved in a variety of ways for use through the winter. Two bushels of flax seed and 40 pounds of flax were produced, which was woven together with wool to produce a 'linsey-woolsey' fabric. In addition, 12 gallons of molasses was produced and beehives provided 50 pounds of honey and 5 pounds of beeswax" (Moretz n.d.:9-11).

By the 1840s a school was serving the children in Plum Tree community; a Methodist church was established around 1850, followed soon after by a Baptist church (Proffit 1984:61).

GRASSY FORK

Not far from Plum Tree, across the ridges in Ashe County, settlement was proceeding in a similar fashion in the Grassy Fork community. Like Plum Tree and Rocky Creek, the community is drained by Grassy Creek, which flows into the Upper New River. Not far from Grassy Fork is the old Buffalo Trail, used by Indians, then white hunters and explorers, before white settlers from the piedmont followed their lead into the mountain valleys in the late 1700s in order to establish permanent homesteads.

Early settlers in the grassy Fork area supplemented their food supplies by hunting and later, as farmsteads were established and land cleared for livestock, "by taking bacon, lard and feathers to Salisbury and Charlotte and [exchanging] them for sugar, salt, cloth, coffee, and other necessities which were not found in the rough area." This area of the state was known as the "Lost Provinces" because of the terrain, the difficulty of transportation, and the paucity of roads, a condition that continued well into the twentieth century. Yet the soil was fertile, the population grew, and self-sufficient community life was achieved through development of the variety of businesses needed to serve the population; a nearby community boasted a "sawmill, grist mill, blacksmith shop, general store, doctor's office, law office, boot and shoe shop, harness and saddle shop, cheese factory, brickyard, tanyard, school, seminary, and at one time a post office" (McKesson 1984:54).

In describing both the terrain and the economic potential of the county, Thomas McGimsey wrote in 1811:

> Great part of Ashe County is mountainous and hilly, yet the soil is extremely rich, yielding an abundance of wheat, rye, oats, barley and buckwheat and other vegetables equal to any cold country on earth.
>
> This is a fine county for pasture and meadows, from which great numbers of cattle and sheep are raised which bring much wealth to the farmer. The air is pure and the water is good, if not superior to any on earth. People live long in Ashe County.
>
> The face of the county is clothed with large and lofty timber of black walnut, sugar tree maple, buckeye, hickory, chestnut, and spruce pine. Clover, strawberries and blue grapes are natural to grow everywhere. Cranberries also in great plenty.

Possibly with an eye to the land-development market, McGimsey adds, "The lands in Ashe County sell for five dollars to five cents per acre" (quoted in Fletcher 1963:13-14).

Mountain communities were defined by the terrain, separated from each other by ridges; property lines generally followed the ridge lines. These ownership and settlement patterns reinforced community identity within hollows and coves and led to a sense of distinctiveness of the various hollow communities. Geographical boundaries defined the lines of frequent communication, and shared experiences, common ancestry, kinship ties, and mutual assistance bound families together and gave them a sense of community (Beaver 1976). While small commercial settlements developed at the mouth of hollows and gaps, towns were widely scattered, and the small-farm economy inhibited the development of a elaborate social hierarchy. Egalitarian values predominated in the interaction of neighbor and kin. While mountain elites emerged from the group of large landowners who provided the political leadership and dominated in local business enterprises, they "did not acquire the power or influence of their counterparts in the rest of the South. The prevalence of small-scale agriculture limited the number and wealth of mountain elites and placed greater social power in the larger yeoman farmer class" (Eller 1982:11-12).

Because of the mountainous terrain, the settlement patterns of dispersed small communities, and the resulting limited transportation networks, the southern and central Appalachians maintained a diversified, small-farm agricultural base longer than other areas of the American South.

Few areas of the United States in the late nineteenth century more closely exemplified Thomas Jefferson's vision for a democratic society than did the agricultural communities of the southern Appalachians. Long after the death of Jefferson and long after the nation as a whole had turned down the Hamiltonian path toward industralism, the southern Appalachians remained a land of small farms and scattered open-country villages. Although traditional patterns of agricultural life persisted in other parts of the nation—in the rural South, the mid-West, and the more remote sections of the northeast—nowhere did the self-sufficient family so dominate the culture and social system as it did in the Appalachian South. [Eller 1982:3]

The Civil War was particularly unsettling to western North Carolina, as internal divisions pitted neighbor against neighbor and divided families, communities, and counties. While young men volunteered and were mustered out to serve the Confederacy in Yancey, Watauga, and Ashe counties, Union sentiment was also strong in each, and an unknown number of men openly or surreptitiously left the state in order to join the Union army. Others sympathetic to the Union but "unwilling to fight against their fellow Southerners . . . avoided enlisting in either army, and when they were in danger of being conscripted, many of them hid in the hills to become known then as 'outliers' " (Blackmun 1977:337).

The most important of many sources of conflict was the issue of slavery. In Yancey County in 1860 there were 375 slaves in a total population of 8,500; they were primarily

concentrated in the southern part of the county, where less
severe terrain was conducive to large landholdings. In 1861,
the portion of Yancey County lying north and east of the Toe
River was divided from Yancey to form the new county of
Mitchell, in which there were strong Union sentiments.
(Other issues, including fair representation in government,
were equally significant in the split.) Yet recruits for both
armies were drawn from both counties.

Ashe County had 533 slaves in a total population of about
8,000. While the first call for volunteers for the Confederate
army was received with great enthusiasm," Ashe County had
many citizens who were opposed to slavery and who pre-
ferred to remain loyal to the Union" (Fletcher 1963:139-40).
One very important result of the local conflict was the split in
local church denominations. "Out of the great Baptist
Church come the Union Baptist, and their churches continue
to this day. The Methodists split in the same way, establishing separate conferences" (Fletcher 1963:140).

Along the New River in Ashe County, pro-Union bush-
whackers from Johnson County, Tennessee, crossed into
Ashe and terrorized Confederate sympathizers. At the same
time, "the 'Homeguard' hung Union sympathizers" on the
North Fork of the New River, on which Grassy Fork is located
(Parker 1975:16-17). While Union sentiment was concentrated along portions of the North Fork in the western portion
of the county, Confederate sentiment was stronger in the
east. This configuration is reflected to this day in the predominance of Republicans on the North Fork and of Democrats in the eastern part of the county.

In Watauga County, Plum Tree sent many of its young men
to serve in the Confederate cause, and as in all of the mountain counties, the war brought great hardships. "The burden
of farming fell upon the women, the old, and the infirm;
renegades made raids through the region periodically, taking
anything they wanted. The news from the war was discourag-
ing" (Proffitt 1984:61). Throughout the mountains, the war
was a time of deprivation, disease (particularly smallpox),
high taxation, and poverty. Yancey County had become
"infested with deserters who either had had enough of war or

who planned at the first opportunity to pass through the lines and join the Union army," as well as a rising number of Union sympathizers "who were ready to join the Federal armies as the quickest means of ending the war" (Deyton 1947:464). Thus, in December 1862 the county refused to send any more men into service of the Confederate cause, and in January 1863 the home guard was formed. However, "the activities of this organization against the bands of robbers and deserters made fast and permanent a hatred among neighbors which was more enduring than the hatred of the enemy" (Deyton 1947:465). As for maintaining order, the home guard was weak and, at best, ineffective. The brigadier general of the North Carolina Guard for Home Defense wrote on April 12, 1864:

> On the Sunday night before a band of tories . . . numbering about 75 men, had surprised the small guard he had left at Burnsville, and broken open the magazine and removed all the arms and ammunition. They had also broken open Brayley's store, and carried off the content; . . . On the day before, a band of about fifty white women of the county assembled together and marched in a body to a store-house near David Proffitt's where they "pressed"—appropriated—about sixty bushels of government wheat, which they carried off. He adds: "The county is gone up. It has got to be impossible to get any man out there unless he is dragged out, with but very few exceptions . . . to call out any more home guards at this time is only certain destruction to the county eventually. In fact, it seems to me, that there is a determination of the people in the county generally to do no more service in the cause. Swarms of man liable to conscription are gone to the tories or to the Yankees . . . while many others are fleeing east of the Blue Ridge for refuge. [Arthur 1973:604]

Deyton writes that following the war "there was a great deal of mistreatment of the vanquished and hatreds were engendered that were to continue for almost half a century. A new political alignment was to come about following geographical lines, with the northern section lining up with the Radical party [and Republicans] and the southern section remaining as a rule loyal to the party of Jackson [and Democrats]" (Deyton 1947:466). The end of the war left Mitchell and Yancey counties torn by political strife that was to last well into the twentieth century and that would provide the basis for party divisions over one hundred years later.

The end of the war left western North Carolina devastated. In Plum Tree, as elsewhere, "the close of the war ended the raids and their attendant dangers to the community, but living conditions remained very much the same. The killing of the Confederate money was a blow to some, particularly the wives or parents of men who sent home part of their Army pay, and the soldiers returned home penniless" (Proffitt 1984:61).

While recovery was slow and the wounds deep, "people learned to help each other as never before; it was now that log rollings, corn chuckings, bean stringings, and molasses making became an integral part of community life." The Plum Tree community "remained an isolated community until the end of the century. There were few additions to the population from the outside, and most of these came from adjacent communities and married into local families" (Proffitt 1984:61).

In the aftermath of the Civil War, the small black populations in the rural mountain counties began to change. In Ashe County, "by the year 1870, several black communities began to emerge" (Parker 1975:18). Through purchase or gift from former slave owners, some black families began to acquire land and to farm, supplementing their income with work for their white neighbors. Others were tenant farmers and sharecroppers. Each of the five black communities in Ashe County "had its leader or spokesman. Whites dealing with blacks on an official basis consulted with the community leader rather than individuals within the community. Early leaders were most often the community preacher or a prosperous landowner" (Parker 1975:19). Similar patterns developed in

Watauga County, where some black families had owned land before the war.

After 1880, however, the Ashe County black population of 963 began to decline as out-migration for work, particularly to the coalfields of West Virginia and elsewhere, began in earnest. Following World War I, more black residents left the county in search of work, and the gradual decline in the percentage of blacks in the county has continued (Parker 1975). The one family still resident in the Grassy Fork township in the 1950s has finally departed, leaving no blacks now in the Grassy Fork area. Watauga and Yancey counties have similar patterns of small black communities, characterized by continuing poplulation fluctuation; no blacks currently reside in either the Plum Tree or the Rocky Creek communities.

The turn of the century witnessed a rapid increase in the value of timber and a steadily growing market for the Southern Appalachian hardwoods. Previously, the small local industry had been dominated by the local subsistence farmer. However, dwindling supplies of timber in New England states during the late nineteenth century brought northern lumbermen and capital investments in the industry to the southern Appalachians, and timbering on a larger scale began in earnest (Price 1901:361).

The railroad finally connected Yancey County, and thus the Rocky Creek area, to the rest of the state and to more distant places by about 1905 (Van Noppen and Van Noppen 1973:265). Timber and mining booms in the county followed the coming of the railroad, which provided the first means for transporting goods out of the mountains.

In 1915 the first train arrived in West Jefferson in Ashe County, and "every mountainside timber boundary became an instant source of cash income. . . . Land prices advanced; the county tax base expanded. For the first time, the 'lost province' was readily open to the outside world, particularly to the north and east" (Duvall 1984:28). Prior to 1915, Ashe County residents had traveled to North Wilkesboro in order

to make rail connections. "[North Wilkesboro] lived off of us
for so very long as all our produce was hauled there. It used to
be said that Ashe County made North Wilkesboro. We went
there to sell about all we had to sell. At that time the
chestnuts hauled there made quite an item. The chickens,
turkeys, eggs, livestock, and grain went there. How good we
felt to have our produce loaded on our own railroad" (Goodman 1977:67).

The railroad reached Watauga County in 1919, followed by
the first hard-surfaced roads by about 1925 (Moretz 1979:56).
Railroads opened up commercial possibilities for marketing
surplus farm products. Up to that time, produce had been
hauled by wagon on poor roads, while "the only market for
livestock was for animals that could be driven out of the area"
(Moretz 1979:56). The Watauga County rail line (known as
the "Tweetsie Railroad"), like the other lines into the mountains, was built at the instigation of the burgeoning lumber
industry. A second railroad connected the northern part of
Watauga County with Abingdon, Virginia, and provided a
nearby depot for sale of crossties by Plum Tree sawyers (Moretz n.d.:29).

Before the railroads came, the groundwork had been laid
for a mineral boom in the Yancey County area, involving the
extraction of mica, kaolin, feldspar, asbestos, and clay. Iron
was mined in the area by the 1820s (Van Noppen and Van
Noppen 1973:351), but during the 1870s the value of rich
deposits of mica was beginning to be realized in the county.
The first mica mines were opened and run by two investors
from outside the region. Two of their mines yielded a total of
$250,000 from about 1820 until 1896 (Shepperd 1935:101).
Mica had been used locally for windowpanes and stove fronts
but began to be transported out of the region by wagon for use
as stove fronts and mica washers as local residents learned
that they could sell it. Shepperd writes of the fervor created
by this new source of income:

> With the opening of the first mines, men accustomed to
> living from the soil and trading hams, honey, sorghum,
> and corn, for salt, coffee, and snuff, came suddenly to

know the feel of quick money. All up and down the Toe
River they burrowed furiously in the earth in untim-
bered, dangerous tunnels that were no more than overgrown groundhog holes, until a cloud of dust seemed to
hang over the mountains. Land holders wanted to know
the exact location of boundary lines and discovered that
ever since the huge colonial grants, men had been buying and selling with bland indifference to exactitude.
There was endless litigation, sometimes bloodshed.
[Shepperd 1935:107]

Bulletin no. 740 of the Department of the Interior estimated
that most of the 400,000 pounds of mica extracted in North
Carolina from 1868 until 1882 came from a few large mines
of the company organized by the two investors mentioned
above (Shepperd 1935:102). Other mines were opened by large
investors on land that had been sold to settlers in the region,
the mineral rights of which had been retained by the original
owners. Some companies purchased large tracts of land; others secured the mineral rights to land whose residents retained the surface ownership, and some leased the land.

Iron mining in Ashe County was likewise affected by the
coming of the railroad. Iron was mined in Ashe County as
early as 1802, and "for more than 80 years the manufacture of
iron was an important industry in Ashe and Alleghany, where
12 or more ironworks, mostly forges, were erected. Some
were washed away in less than ten years; some were rebuilt;
some were abandoned; and one was operated part of the year
for about 70 years" (Holbrook 1984:16).

While the Civil War saw a surge in mining, as "tons of iron
from the Ashe and Alleghany forges helped the Confederate
cause" (Holbrook 1984:15), iron mining was abandoned after
the war. "In 1896 there were no mines nor forges in operation—only blacksmiths hammering the iron into nails and
tools, 13 in Ashe and two in Alleghany." The coming of the
railroad caused a new surge of activity, although "by 1922 this
activity had ceased," so that "ironmining became a forgotten
industry along the New River in North Carolina" (Holblrook
1984:16).

Resort land speculation and development had begun to affect western North Carolina in a limited way during the early to mid nineteenth century. "From early days, the cool climate and scenic mountains of the Blue Ridge were sought as a haven from the heat and the illnesses thought to be caused by the unfavorable climate of the lowlands. Many people built summer homes in Blowing Rock, which is still largely a resort community, as early as the 1850's" (Moretz 1980:99). Hendersonville had become a popular place for families from Charleston and Savannah to spend the summer, as a haven from both heat and disease. "Although many of the visitors built fine homes in towns . . . , a good number spent the summer in boarding houses. The management and construction of these houses served as forerunners of the modern tourist industry in western North Carolina" (Efird 1980:3).

The railroads provided the means for developing the variety of mountain industries, including the recreation industry. In Asheville, for example, following completion of the railroad the population doubled between 1880 and 1885—from 2,600 to more than 5,000—and by 1890, the population had reached over 11,500 permanent residents, with an estimated 30,000 summer people who traveled from the lowlands on the railroads (Langley and Langley 1975:32-36).

The population of other rural counties in western North Carolina also increased steadily during the early decades of this century. For example, Yancey County grew from 5,000 in 1870 to 11,000 in 1900, 12,000 in 1910, and 15,000 in 1930; the population peaked at 17,000 in 1940. Similarly, the population of Ashe County was highest in the census year 1940, with 22,664 inhabitants. As in the rest of southern Appalachia, the population of Appalachian North Carolina grew during the period 1900 to 1950 (from 366,948 to 683,931), nearly doubling. Recreational land use also developed significantly during the period, including the acquisition of lands for public use. "The formation of the Great Smoky Mountains National Park and the construction associated with the Tennessee Valley Authority system and the Blue Ridge Parkway brought new people into the region" (Efird 1980:3). Local supporters in the "Boone and Asheville areas won the contest with Tennessee for the route of the Blue Ridge Parkway in 1934. The Parkway, which runs through the southern part of [Watauga] county, served as a convenient and attractive avenue to bring more tourist commerce into the county, and still serves as a strong stimulus for continued recreational development" (Moretz 1980:100).

In the decades following World War II, the population throughout southern Appalachia declined significantly. The Great Migration is well documented, as the rate of migration from the region was 13.1 percent between 1940 and 1950 and 19 percent between 1950 and 1960 (Brown and Hillery 1962:58). These population declines were echoed in Ashe and Yancey Counties, whose populations declined 1 percent and 5 percent between 1940 and 1950 and 10 percent and 14 percent between 1950 and 1960. Population shifts in Watauga County during this time reflect an increase of 1 percent between 1940 and 1950 and a slight decline of 4 percent between 1950 and 1960. During the years 1960 to 1970, while the Ashe County population continued to decline slightly by 1 percent and the Yancey County population by 10 percent, the Watauga County population experienced a dramatic increase of 33.5 percent, reflecting the local "boom in university and recreation growth. . . . This growth was the highest of any county in Region D (a seven county planning area), three times the North Carolina growth rate (+10.4%), and 12 times the Appalachian rate (+2.7%)" (Moretz 1980:101).

Western North Carolina as a whole, while feeling the impact of the out-migration that was occurring throughout the region, continued to gain population during the 1950s, "but at a much slower rate than the national rate of 18%. The absence of massive out-migration in North Carolina reflected less reliance on primary extractive industries, such as coal mining often found elsewhere in the mountains, and more emphasis on a diversified small farm economy. The economic situation in North Carolina never became as serious as that in other southern Appalachian states and people remained in their native areas of western North Carolina" (Efird 1980:3-4).

Population shifts within each of these three counties between 1960 and 1970 reflect a national trend of movement from rural farm toward rural nonfarm and urban residence. While the Ashe County population declined by 1 percent and Yancey by 10 percent, the rural townships in which Grassy Fork and Rocky Creek are located continued to decline by 8 percent and 30 percent, reflecting population shifts within these predominantly rural counties. The Watauga County population grew by a whopping 33.5 percent between 1960 and 1970, reflecting primarily a growth in the areas surrounding the two incorporated townships in the county, Boone and Blowing Rock, "due in part to student growth at Appalachian State Univerity and annexation" (Moretz 1980:101). The other Watauga County townships either lost population (3 percent for the one including Plum Tree) or gained only by small percentages.

Between 1970 and 1980, changing economic conditions in western North Carolina, including industrial development and, particularly, the land development boom, had major effects on the population there, including the counties of Ashe, Watauga, and Yancey. While each of the county populations grew (Ashe County by 14 percent, Watauga by 35 percent, and Yancey by 18 percent), the rural township populations made great population gains as well (Grassy Fork by 9 percent, Plum Tree by 47 percent, and Rocky Creek by 37 percent). These changes reflect the decline in out-migration, coupled with dramatic increase in both return migration and migration of new residents into the rural areas. Several factors have been proposed to account for this regionwide trend in migration reversal, including "industrial growth and, more specifically . . . the growth of nontraditional kinds of industries that require greater investment of skill levels (like machinery and chemicals rather than textiles). Additionally, gains are attributed to the development of retirement and recreation-oriented communities, to the preference by many to reside in nonmetropolitan areas, to kinship ties, and to rapidly rising unemployment in many northern cities. The population turnaround is also related to greatly improved accessibility to both metropolitan counties, which have jobs, and nonmetropolitan counties, which have homes, within the region." (Raitz and Ulack 1984:171). With the addition of the university in Watauga County, each of these explantions is appropriate to Ashe, Watauga, and Yancey counties.

MANUFACTURING INDUSTRIES

Following the timber and mineral interests into the South, manufacturing concerns, attracted by the availability of a cheap labor force, began establishing factories on the mountain fringes. Between 1900 and 1930, over six hundred company towns sprang up in the southern Appalachians, drawing mountain families from the farm and into factory towns (Eller 1982). By the 1940s and 1950s, small textile mills had begun to locate in the rural counties in the mountains. Two textile mills opened in Yancey County during the 1950s, soon to be followed by other such concerns, providing new opportunities for employment on a local basis. In 1950, 5 percent of those employed in Yancey County were working in manufacturing. By 1960 this figure had risen to 30 percent, and by 1970, to 45 percent. In 1970, of the 1,900 people employed in manufacturing, 1,300 worked in local textile mills. Estimates for 1985 reveal a similar pattern, with a slight decline; of the 1,800 employees in industry, approximately 1,210 work in one of the seven textile mills in the county. Glen Raven Mills is the largest textile employer, with 358 employees, followed by Avondale Mills with 300 and Pacemaker with 225. Despite the seven textile plants and the five other industries—two small mining concerns (57 employees), one lumberyard (55 employees), a bedding springs factory (115 employees), and an outboard motor manufacturer (330 employees)—employment opportunities in the county remain limited, so that an estimated "40 percent of the work force must commute outside of the county for employment," according to the county Chamber of Commerce.

In Ashe County after World War II, "small industry began to flourish—wood products such as flooring and chairs; sawmilling; soft drink bottling; and the marketing of livestock, beans, and tobacco. Ashe County's farmers operated two hundred small dairies using Coble, Kraft, and Yadkin Valley as purchasing and marketing organizations. More money came into circulation from individual enterprise and initiative. Rural electric service lifted the burden of daily toil" (Duvall 1984:30).

By the midthirties, Phoenix Chair Manufacturing Company had begun operation with a few employees in Ashe County. Expanded and operating as Thomasville Furniture Company, it provided employment for 400 county residents in 1984. In 1953, Peerless Hosiery Company opened in West Jefferson and has since expanded as Southern Devices, manufacturing electronic equipment and employing 430 people. A third major employer is Sprague Electric Company, a manufacturer of electric capacitors, with 565 employees. The largest employer in the county, however, is Hanes, a textile manufacturer with 610 employees. Another textile manufacturer, Jefferson Apparel, has 310 employees. Other smaller companies operate in the county; one of the oldest commercial concerns in the county, Ashe County Cheese, continues to use the products of local dairies and in 1984 had 35 employees. (Data provided by Ashe County Chamber of Commerce.)

Watauga County's economic development was heavily influenced by the presence of Appalachian State University. Founded as Watauga Academy in 1899, the college experienced periods of dramatic growth, particularly after becoming part of the University of North Carolina consolidated system in 1967. Besides being the largest single employer in the county, employing approximately 1,500 faculty, staff, and students, the university attracts approximately 10,000 students—a significant number for Watauga County.

The movement of industry into the mountains also occurred in Watauga County, beginning in the 1950s with International Resistance Company in 1956 and Shadowline (maker of ladies' lingerie) in 1957. In the 1960s, Blue Ridge Shoe began operations, as did Vermont American (a manufacturer of sawblades). A local canning factory, specializing in cannning sauerkraut made from locally grown cabbage, had operated since the 1920s, but with the decline in agricultural activity in the 1970s, the plant finally closed; the building, after changing hands, was eventually taken over by American Wicker, now producing wicker and wood products. Other small industries, several locally owned, also were developing during the 1960s and 1970s, to be joined by still others in the late 1970s and early 1980s. The impact of the declining United States textile industry affected the county, however, with a reduction in the number of employees at Shadowline (from 483 in 1977 to 310 in 1985) and the 1977 closing of Blue Ridge Shoe, which had employed 280 people. In the 1980s, industry is a basis of the Watauga County economy, with thirteen companies employing 1,800 people, as estimated by the Chamber of Commerce in 1985.

The tourism industry in Watauga County has continued to grow during the early 1980s and in 1985 accounted for approximately 2,000 jobs. Approximately 1.5 million tourists visit the area annually; in 1983 the Chamber of Commerce estimated that they spent over spent over $54.6 million. With the county's industrial development, dramatic population increase, and tourism has come the opening of a new shopping center, having an estimated county retail sales figure of $236 million.

The opening of new industries in the rural mountain counties began an important trend in the local and family economy and in the social system, namely, the increasing participation of women in the labor force. In Yancey County, for example, women composed only about 11 percent of the labor force in 1940; this figure had risen to 20 percent in 1950, 25 percent in 1960, 33 percent in 1970, and 45 percent in 1980. Similar patterns reflect the new job opportunities that existed in Ashe and Watauga counties with the opening of new plants, particularly since the 1950s. In Ashe and Watauga, women made up 46 percent and 47 percent of the labor force in 1980, with the majority of women employed in industries, in retail trade, and as service professionals, particularly teachers.

AGRICULTURE

The move away from agriculture is another significant trend in rural counties in western North Carolina. This decline to a large extent reflects the national decline in small farms due

to "decreasing farm prices, increasing production costs and
interest rates, and increased mechanization and technology
by large agri-business farms [that] have made it difficult for
the small farmer to compete" (Moretz 1979:57). In western
North Carolina, however, the additional factor of the developing recreation and second-home industry has had a major
impact on landownership, land use, and land prices and has
accelerated the decline in agriculture. Between 1969 and
1974, for example, Ashe County experienced a 36 percent
loss in the number of farms, with a loss of 33,010 acres of
farmland. Watauga County lost 30 percent of its farms, a
decline by 12,338 in its farm acreage. At the same time,
tourism services grew by 12.5 percent in Ashe County, and
the number of second-home purchases was high; Watauga
County's tourism services produced 64 percent of the county's service receipts during this same period (Appalachian
Land ownership Task Force 1983:87). Changing landownership patterns affect agriculture by creating "land speculation and a price escalation that puts land prices far above
what the local market can bear. "Land values in relatively
undeveloped agricultural townships of Watauga County
(North Carolina), for example, increased an average of 225%
in the twelve-year period from 1963 to 1975" (ALOTF
1983:88). The relationship between expansion of the tourism
and recreation industry, high land prices, and the decline in
agriculture is apparent throughout recreation areas of the
southern Appalachians. High land prices "may tempt people
to sell, and thereby put land out of agricultural use. They act
as a barrier to expansion of farms or to new farmers entering
the occupation (unless they have been fortunate enough to
inherit a plot of land). Property taxes soar to meet new services demanded by the tourist economy" (ALOTF 1983:88). In
these counties, where farmers turn to other occupations,
young families cannot afford to purchase land and equipment
in order to enter farming.

While agriculture is on the decline in western North Carolina, it nevertheless accounts for a percentage of each county's economy. In 1980, people employed in agriculture represented 7 percent of the employed labor force in Ashe County,

4 percent in Watauga, and 3 percent in Yancey. The proportion of county land in farms in 1982 was 47 percent in Ashe, 28 percent in Watauga, and 27 percent in Yancey. The average size of farms in 1982 was eighty-six acres in Ashe County, sixty-three in Watauga, and sixty-four in Yancey. In 1984, agricultural income in Watauga County was $19.2 million, with approximately two-thirds coming from beef cattle, poultry, and tobacco and one-third from horticultural crops (Chamber of Commerce estimate). In Ashe County, farm receipts amounted to almost $24 million in 1984 (Center for Improving Mountain Living 1984).

While the percentage of farm workers in Watauga County is small, the growing of ornamentals and Christmas trees is becoming an important new source of income and is less labor-intensive than traditional agricultural activities. "During the 1970s the agricultural sector was shifting from complete reliance on annual crops to an emphasis on these new crops . . . this market-oriented sector can be assumed to be a continuing and important part of the county's economy" (League of Women Voters 1984:6).

Occupations of residents of the Rocky Creek, Plum Tree, and Grassy Fork communities range from total dependence on agriculture to total dependence on nonagricultural sources of income, with the majority of residents falling somewhere in between. Despite a dramatic decline in agriculture over the last forty years, agricultural activities remain important sources of both food and income to supplement wage labor for many residents of the three communities. Wage labor is the primary source of income in each community, yet agriculture provides an important economic margin. Many families in the three communities grow their tobacco allotment and truck garden a variety of crops including tomatoes, beans, squash, cabbage, corn, potatoes, onions, cucumbers, and apples. Dairying is an occupation for one family each in Rocky Creek and in Grassy Fork, where beef cattle is also a major income source for several families. Beef cattle provides a small source of supplementary income or meat to several other families in each of the three communities, who also keep a few pigs, sheep, chickens (for meat and for eggs), and other fowl, including ducks, turkeys, guineas, and geese. Several families in each community keep horses as well; horseback riding is a popular Sunday afternoon activity.

While the decline of agriculture is characteristic of each of the three communities, tobacco remains an important income source for many rural mountain residents. Burley tobacco was introduced to the Appalachian Mountains by 1923 (Van Noppen and Van Noppen 1973:277) and is a type of tobacco that can be grown on the small farm with limited land and limited equipment. As compared with flue-cured tobacco grown in eastern and central parts of North Carolina, the entire burley plant is harvested at one time and allowed to dry before the leaves are stripped from the stalk and sorted according to quality. Burley tobacco is harvested later than flue-cured tobacco and is sold at nearby auctions during the fall and even for a few days after Christmas. Allotments on the amount of tobacco allowed per acre were introduced in 1948 (Van Noppen and Van Noppen 1973:279) and are currently the subject of debate in Congress.

Tobacco farming in rural Appalachian communities has proven particularly adaptable to the fluctuating mountain economy, since "many of the farmers now work away from their farms and fit the chores connected with their tobacco crop into evening and Saturday work. . . . Tobacco is well-suited to part time farming" (Van Noppen and Van Noppen 1973:280). Tobacco is an important supplementary source of income for many rural families. Those with adequate land raise their own allotment or rent their allotment to others who either do not own allotments or wish to raise a larger amount of tobacco than a single alltoment allows.

In the few full-time farming families, most of the men have worked for pay on jobs for other community residents or have worked in public jobs, and most have "swapped work" with neighbors. Women in these families have also joined the public work force, and in several families, the wife's job in the public sector provides the economic margin that allows the family farm or dairy to continue.

Approximately half of the households in each community are neither totally dependent on agriculture nor totally dependent on public work but meet their families' needs with income from public work, full-time or seasonal, supplemented by sale of cash crops (including tobacco and truck garden produce) and by the products of kitchen gardens. Work in the public sector varies somewhat from community to community because of the types of positions available in nearby towns. Plum Tree and Grassy Fork are located within twenty and forty-five minutes' drive of the university, and several men and women from each community are employed on the staff or faculty, enjoying the valued benefits associated with those positions. A majority of the women in each of the three communities employed in the public sector are blue-collar workers in light industries, while others work in retail sales, in the county hospital, in social services agencies, in county government, or on clerical positions in local businesses. Each community boasts at least one public-school teacher.

Men commonly find work in a wider variety of industries, small businesses and government agencies as mechanics, welders, carpenters, custodians, electricians, or plumbers. Yet a few in each community drive long distances each day to blue-collar jobs in industries, carpooling with neighbors.

While migration from southern Appalachia, particularly after World War II, resulted in a population decline that slowed only in the 1970s, temporary out-migration has been characteristic of some families and many of the men of the communities. Work histories of older men are quite varied, often including work in timber in a place as far away as Oregon (common in Grassy Fork), work in mining in eastern Kentucky, southwest Virginia, Georgia, South Carolina, and Tennessee or work in various industries in the Northeast.

Brown, Schwarzweller, and Mangalam (1963) and others have demonstrated the importance of extended-family ties with respect to migration destinations. People often migrate to places where they have kin to help ease them through the adjustment period. Thus in Rocky Creek, knowledge of specific locales in Ohio and Maryland is often greater than that of eastern North Carolina. In Grassy Fork, people are familiar

with Oregon and Pennsylvania; kin reside there still, returning occasionally to visit.

The expansion of the tourism and recreation industries,
particularly during the mid-1960s, created new job opportunities for men in the communities. However, jobs available
in these areas are generally seasonal and low wage; new
building ventures related to an expanded second-home market have likewise provided some jobs, particularly for back-
to-the-land men, though again these are seasonal and temporary, ending with the completion of the house or development. Work may be found in associated businesses, such as
materials supply companies and concrete and gravel plants;
for women, a few clerical positions are available in these and
in real estate offices.

Most middle-aged and older men have significant work
experience in timbering and sawmilling, although the timber
boom has long since passed and, along with it, all of the virgin
timber in southern Appalachia. A few men in each community are sawyers, one each in Rocky Creek and Plum Tree
running sawmills. Several others own portable sawmills,
used in sawing lumber for local sale. Landowners occasionally sell a few trees or log a portion of their timber for sale to
local companies; in this way the lumber industry provides a
small additional income to a few families on an irregular
basis, besides the full-time employment for the few.

While the university employs several men in the Grassy
Fork and Plum Tree communities, mining has provided jobs
for several men in Rocky Creek. Most of the mica used in the
United States has come from the area near Rocky Creek,
which at times has been the chief area in the United States for
the production of clay, mica, and feldspar. Yet mica, like
timbering, was in the past often mined by one or two individuals who decided to try their luck with small operations on
their own property. Thus many men in Rocky Creek have, at
one time or another, worked in mining and related activities,
such as trucking. The mining industry, however, provides
little economic input to Rocky Creek, affecting the income of
a few individuals in processing and another few involved in
trucking. Several Rocky Creek and Grassy Fork families are

involved in trucking goods for a variety of local industries, and other men have worked on a more or less regular basis for these neighbors or have driven for a trucking firm.

The approximately 180 years since the nineteenth-century settlers arrived in these rural western North Carolina communities can be characterized over the first hundred years by the gradual development of largely self-sufficient, self-contained agricultural communities. While subsistence agriculture predominated, local artisans and specialists provided necessary services to their communities as millers, sawyers, blacksmiths, spinners, weavers, cabinetmakers (and perhaps casket makers), carpenters, sometimes teachers and preachers, musicians, storytellers, healers and herbalists, and the occasional lawyer or scholar. Trade of goods in market centers was difficult but worthwhile for obtaining goods otherwise unavailable. Following the devastation of the Civil War, the timber industry's push to complete rail links between the mountain counties and market centers had a profound impact on regional economic and social conditions. Not only was the timber sold (which in itself had a major, if somewhat short-lived, impact on local economies and a radical impact on the mountain ecology) but agricultural products and people were carried out as well. While cousins in nearby locales could be visited with ease, business could be transacted in distant cities, and young men could go west to seek their fortunes, with a few returning to farm the homeplace.

The last eighty years have seen the decreasing self-reliance of the rural communities and their increasing integration into an industrial order that is growing more and more complex. The rail lines brought in new residents who, along with developers of the recreation industry, were attracted to the region by the mild and invigorating climate and by the scenic beauty. Major changes in landownership, land use, population composition, and local economies resulted from the gradual expansion of the tourism and recreation industries into the boom periods of the 1960s and 1970s.

Industrial growth and development, beginning in the 1950s and accelerating since the mid-1970s, provided economic alternatives to the decreasingly viable agricultural economy, the seasonal tourism industry, or out-migration. Meanwhile, land prices and land values in all but the most remote areas of the mountains have skyrocketed, making it virtually impossible for local young people to begin farming as an occupation and also slowing down the back-to-the-land movement of the early to mid 1970s. While the population of rural communities continues a steady increase, most new residents are buying smaller parcels, settling for an attractive physical setting, the option of gardening, and a place in a social system rather than for large acreage for farming purposes.

With these changes, especially in communities like Plum Tree, close enough to a growing urban area to provide accessible housing, have come a new measure of prosperity and a greater demand for services—like prompt snow removal, better road maintenance, and the beginnings of cable television. Social stratification is a significant feature of the rural mountain community and will, no doubt, become even more important in the coming decades as agriculture continues to decline in importance, as public work opportunities become more prevalent, as land prices continue to exclude local young people from the land market, and as newcomers continue to alter the nature of local social and economic relationships.[2] At the same time, older styles of relating as neighbor to neighbor are still operating but are indeed changing; some will no doubt disappear in the next few decades. The next chapters explore some of these social patterns and value systems as they function in the 1980s, each with a historic precedent but with perhaps an uncertain future.

Chapter Two

THE FLOOD

NOVEMBER 1977

After a week of dreary weather, Saturday morning brought the promise of yet another day of rain. That morning the rain began quietly, softly, yet steadily, the sounds blending with the regular chattering of streams that coursed through the community. By late afternoon, it had become a steady, unrelenting downpour, sheets of rain beating like hail against windowpanes and tin roofs. Bare tree limbs bent low in the gale, as twigs and small branches swirled through the air and littered the ground. By early evening the few cars with returning shoppers and shift workers moved slowly along the road, headlights piercing short distances through the torrents and windshield wipers failing to provide much visibility to the cautious occupants. Yet still the rain came. Through the evening and well into the long night, its pounding was the only sound. Shortly before midnight, the rain finally slackened, yet more ominous sounds continued in its place: the roar of rivulets become swift creeks, creeks become rivers, and the river itself become a torrent.

As dawn began to replace the all-encompassing darkness, the picture of the night's destruction slowly started to unfold. The river had become a sea of frothing whitecaps, tumbling along the refuse from normally high trash piles like abandoned toys, together with logs, a pigpen, bridge timbers ripped loose from pilings, and plastic milk jugs. Each passing object crashed into other objects or into the river bank and tore at the now-dwarfed supports on the massive steel bridge linking part of the community with the two-lane highway.

Most houses on Rocky Creek were safe on high ground, yet the families had spent a fitful night. Some had watched and checked and shuffled equipment and livestock during the drenching. A few on lower ground had spent the hours after midnight battling rising waters that were flooding across the doorsills. As the dawn began to break, each family stirred to begin surveying the night's destruction. How much livestock washed away, how many pole barns trembling and tottering unsupported, which bridges gone, which neighbors in trouble?

Jake wandered out to gaze into the gray morning while Pat put on the coffeepot and began frying bacon. She wanted to call her mother but decided against it. If her parents needed help, they would have called; if they were all right, the early morning call would only upset her aging father. Besides, the house was high above the river, and they would go see for themselves shortly. Instead, she called her sister Caroline, who answered on the first ring, having spent most of the night in anxious waiting. Caroline's husband had returned from the night shift at the mill in Burnsville as the river was rising, and he reported that, though the road was threatened, the bridge was still safe and Uncle Pontiac's house, which he had glimpsed in the darkness, seemed secure. Down at the other end of the county, where the river was wider and the valley broad and flat with houses strung alongside the road, the threat of disaster was great.

The voices out front drew Pat to the door. Cecil stood dripping on the edge of the porch, telling Jake that J.B. may have lost a few head of cattle but was down on the river with his brother Tom and Tom's sons shoving rock under the washed-out end of his tottering barn. Cecil would return to help him after he checked on Aunt Sarah. He knew she'd be fretful about the house and her grandchildren. He had seen Mrs. Woody out checking on her chickens and her hog, Sue. She said that the culvert that usually carried the little stream under the road and on by her house had clogged, sending the torrent over the road and into her front room. After fighting it for a while, the boys had disgustedly ripped out the culvert with the bulldozer. The road was gone, but the house was saved, and the damage to the house could have been a lot greater.

As Cecil left to go up to Aunt Sarah's, Jake and Pat hurried into the kitchen to drink the hot coffee and to devour the steaming bacon and eggs. The chill of the wet November morning had begun to penetrate their skin, and they cherished the few moments in the warm kitchen. Fortunately, the weather hadn't yet turned too cold, or there would be a lot of sickness as folks worked through this drenching Sunday morning.

As the Chevy pickup inched out the sloshy driveway, the rain subsided even more. No rays of sunlight would appear that day or the next, but the worst was over. The rains had come, they had persisted, but finally they were exhausted. The radio told of tragedy in the whole country—a drowning in Johnson County, a missing wife and child in Buncombe, both feared dead. But despite the midnight evacuations of riverbank houses and the overturned and floating mobile homes, none had been reported lost in the county. The gospel hour and Brother Hardy's pleas for salvation reminded Pat that this day was, after all, a special day of the week and that this crisis would pass.

They rounded the bend and drove past the newly cut road, now slick with red mud, winding into the side of the hill where four new houses perched over the fields below. Only the month before, Ernest Hinkle had sold the last one to a retired couple from Florida. Pat mentioned the Florida houses and wondered how those flimsy structures were weathering the storm. Jake said he didn't care; they could fall in the river as far as he was concerned. Pat noted that "they're takin' our mountains, ever bit of 'em, but them houses are perched up so high on the rocks that no flood would ever bother 'em. They may blow over, but they'll not wash away."

On the way down to Pat's mother's, they neared the driveway to the old Maggie Wiseman place, now owned by the young couple who had come up from Florida. Jake had called them hippies at first, but they seemed nice enough and

worked pretty hard—"that long-haired fellow" had done a lot
of work trying to straighten out the jackleg plumbing other
renters had so thoroughly jumbled. The wife had gotten a job
in town with the health department and had done a good deal
of canning in the evenings and on weekends.

As they neared the house, the younger couple, George and
Carol, appeared on the porch. They hailed Jake and Pat, who
stopped to talk; George and Carol were excited and worried—
their place seemed secure, but what about the folks down the
river? Was the bridge out? How would they get to work and to
the grocery store? They had never seen such rains—would
they cease? Had this happened before? The young couple's
eyes grew wider as Pat talked of the flood of '40. They laughed
that they would be able to tell their grandchildren about the
flood of '77. Pat said that a few real old people could even
remember the flood of '16, but she didn't know too much
about that one.

The young couple asked if they might go along with Jake
and Pat, so the four of them squeezed their rain-drenched
bodies into the cab. The acrid smell of wet rubber boots and
plastic rain gear permeated the cab as the truck eased along
the river road.

A few more vehicles were moving about now, and the
pickup stopped three times before nearing its destination a
mile away. Each passing vehicle shared concerns, new information of near tragedy or rescue, and reassurances, as neighbors hungry for information related their own bits of news.
Each tried to ascertain where they were needed and whether
their kin and neighbors were all right.

Pat's mother's driveway was partially submerged by the
flooding creek, and Jake and George got out to see if the little
bridge was still intact and would bear the load. They finally
decided to try it and spun and swayed through the torrent to
safety on the other, higher side of the road.

Pat scrambled out of the truck when it finally came to a
stop and sloshed her way up to her parents' front door where
her mother, Lizzie, stood. Wet broom in hand, she greeted her
daughter with unusual fatigue. She had spent a restless night,
listening to the thunder and the unseen water rising in the

darkness. She had relished the first light, which had allayed her fears of total destruction yet confirmed her suspicions of trouble. Pat's father had not even stirred. Lizzie had finally wakened him about 6:30 A.M. to tell him of the flooding, and she had laughed at his surprise and disbelief. From the safety of the high front porch, Pat and Lizzie watched the river, not five hundred feet away now, boiling with the debris.

As the others joined the two women, they all turned to the immediate business at hand—the now-flooded cellar. Lizzie's handmade baskets were still high and dry, but the rest of the contents—her canned goods and various tools—were under water. Jake, Pat, Carol, and George began carrying the load into the porch, as Lizzie and old Sam directed the activity.

Two hours later the foursome was back on the road. Pat's sister Caroline and her two oldest children had joined the effort and would stay with the older couple awhile, helping dry things out, straighten up, and comfort the fretting parents.

Cecil had stopped in on his way from Sarah's to report that all was well there, except that Sarah hadn't been able to reach her son down on South Creek. The radio had reported that all the mobile homes in the trailer park in town had been flooded and the families had been evacuated, but no word had yet come to Sarah of her young son's family. Maybe since their home was in the middle of the trailer park it would be all right, but the little baby worried her.

The Chevy fell in behind Cecil's, and the small caravan continued along the river. By the time they reached the farm, J.B. had his tractor out and was moving rock and mud. The barn somehow remained standing. The little spring where the cattle got water had cut a six-foot-deep trench under one side of the barn. George and Jake joined the rock-moving effort as they tried to shore up the side of the barn.

Miraculously, no one had drowned in the county, though many had harrowing tales of near-disaster. Shortly after the water subsided, Aunt Sarah's boys and several neighbors had spent an evening clearing the clogged culvert and putting it back into the creek. It would be months before the county road crews would inspect the well-traveled dirt road. Seven or eight other men temporarily repaired the partially collapsed bridge linking upper Rocky with the rest of the community; the iris would be in full bloom before that structure would be replaced by a new steel and concrete bridge.

For weeks, the flood was the central topic of conversation around public gathering places. A few collections were taken up for neighbors on South Creek who had lost everything. Then the flood relief people and their helicopters came, but most folks on Rocky Creek assumed that such help was for the really bad off folks elsewhere, so only a few visited the Relief Office.

Some folks discussed the flood of '40, when most of the gristmills in the country had been washed away, never to be rebuilt. Competition with Red Band and Marth White had made rebuilding the old family-based structures infeasible, as did the war effort, declining population, and stepped-up production and employment in the local mines and new factories. The economic loss from the '40 flood to the county and especially to individual families had been tremendous. Over in Watauga County, Fred Woody had awakened that morning in 1940 to gaze out upon a slowly moving river grown four times its normal width and covering the whole valley. The silence with which it moved along was more terrifying than the crashing of the creek reaching to within six feet from his house. "I looked out and just could see one stalk of corn yonder sticking out of that water, and beyond it, the top of one 'baccer plant. I lost everything I had that year: five hundred pounds of 'baccer, two hundred bushel of corn, two or three hundred bushel of beans, a thousand head of cabbage. I had some cabbage and 'taters that didn't get flooded up beside the house, but they lay there and rot in the ground 'cause I couldn't get 'em out. Ever bridge in the whole country was gone." But even more tragic was the human suffering throughout the area. Fred observed that "lots of people lost their lives. Law, it was a terrible time." A family downriver who were "a right smart of kin" had all drowned, as had many others.

Some few remembered tales of the flood of '16, but somehow the effects had not seemed so far reaching, or else old memories had been dimmed.

Some discussed the flood of '60, which, more than in the mountains, wreaked havoc in the coastal plains of the state. Cemeteries had been washed away, and coffins rose from the ground. Mountain cemeteries were certainly preferable to the vulnerable lowland ones; their dead could rest without danger of reappearing during periodic flooding. The six family cemeteries in Rocky Creek are all high on hillsides or mountaintop meadows. Some said the dead were closer to God; others said they were protected from troubled water.

Except for an occasional tree limb felled by high winds or lightning and for the lush vegetation that regularly had to be cleared from fragile, fading markers, the cemeteries had never been disturbed by human or natural forces. Side by side lay graves of well-remembered loved ones and ancestors dating back into the early nineteenth century. Each visit to the cemeteries recalled the chronology of life in this place from the days of settlement. Names like Edd, Ott, Theophilus, and Don't triggered jokes and laughter and new questions from the children. Elders would ponder the relationships and would relate notorious events from the lives of these people to whom they were related by blood but whom they had known only through legend. Each grave marker had its own particular, sometimes tragic, story to tell: the young woman who died in childbirth—hardly more than a child herself, she left behind a grieving young husband and a baby daughter to be raised by her parents; the young son struck down in his prime by an accident while cutting timber with his father, leaving behind his grieving parents and new bride; the soldier who died so far from home and family but whose death was honored by his country's funeral ceremony and grave marker.

Months later, though the flood was only rarely discussed, grim reminders remained. Before the damage had been even partially assessed, a winter freeze fixed the surplus ground water into the earth. Bits of plastic and paper fluttered in the winter winds on riverbank trees and bushes, plastic milk jugs were frozen into barnyard mud, and every bend in the river harbored tangled piles of plastic, tires, and pebbles.

The severe winter then prolonged the flood impact well into early summer. Many roads, shaken and torn by the flood itself, erupted during a mid-March thaw, making paved roads treacherous and dirt roads virtually impassable. Despite extra funding, efforts of state and county road crews were insufficient to repair the extensive damage.

Cicero Woody's brother-in-law in Ashe County had won contracts from the federal people to rebuild some of the bridges. After making what he considered to be high estimates, he discovered that an outfit in Jefferson was charging double the fair amount and getting paid for it. So he upped his bills considerably. He felt a little guilty about it at first, but since the federal people seemed such fools and so determined to get rid of the money anyway, he figured they might as well give it to him as to the big-time outfits that didn't need the money.

By early May, seasonal demands had taken priority over any more flood- or winter-repair efforts; what had not been repaired would be ignored, perhaps indefinitely. A few barns would be torn down during the lull of late fall after the tobacco was sold and before the worst of the winter began. Others, like the Buchanans', which had sat lopsided since the flood of '60, when one side had sunk down three feet lower than the other, would remain as they were for another undetermined number of years. The more pressing demands of young calves struggling into the world, a process that had begun early in March, took precedence now. The bawling of the cows whose calves had been separated from them and herded into other pasture continued unabated for several days.

By midsummer, the flood seemed far away indeed. Hollyhocks, daylilies, shades of purple phlox, and white Queen Anne's lace tangled with greens of other roadside vegetation to conceal any flood debris the rains had not removed. The most tangible reminder of the flood was the big new bridge spanning the now-placid river. Summer's extra labor, often squeezed around public jobs into evenings and weekends and around the visiting relatives from Baltimore, Cincinnati, and Dayton, began to show in filling root cellars, basement canning shelves, hay barns, and freezers.

AUGUST 1978

After a gentle, night rain, the air was crystal clear; the colors of the world were intense. The rich brown of the weathered barn stood in striking contrast to the lush greens of mid-August. Despite the heat of midday, the clarity of the air after a week of dog-day's dust reminded Iris that fall would come again. A lone car moved unhurriedly up the road. In the small field adjacent to the house, J.B. lifted the hayfork to turn the hay doused by the previous night's rain. He'd said that it would be certain to rain if he cut the hay; sure enough, the welcome shower had brought enough water to Iris's garden to revive the squash, cucumbers, and peppers. If the hay weren't allowed to dry, it would rot or, worse, catch fire in the barn during the winter. Cecil's lumber truck drove by, carrying a heavy load. Iris waved at his two little boys perched precariously on top of the cab with their backs to the load. Then all was still again. The creek tumbled along quietly in front of the house, while the radio told of drunken love, summer clearance sales, and recapped tires.

Revived from the kitchen heat by the cool of the front porch shaded by the ancient maple tree, Iris went back to her chores. She paused to admire the abundant red geraniums in clay pots on the clean-swept floor. Flanking them were the now-still rockers made for Sunday afternoon and summer evening conversations. She had loved these rockers as a child, when she would rock for hours on her grandparents' porch. They would envelop the little children; the bigger children could rock as hard as they liked with no danger of turning over. When her grandmoter died, three years to the week after her grandfather, her mother saw to it that the rockers went to Iris. Like everything else the Buchanans owned, the rockers were massive and sturdy—made for large, rough people and made to endure. They had been painted numerous times, and their texture was soft but not fragile; they were sturdy but not uncomfortable.

Serena and her two youngest children, Pattie and Charlie, arrived just as Iris was shoving the last piece of wood possible into the cookstove firebox. While Iris adjusted the lid on the pressure canner for the first run of beans, Serena poured herself a cup of coffee, settled down at the kitchen table across the room, and reached for a handful of half runners from the bushel basket on the floor. The crop had been extremely prolific, and the sisters-in-law had spent the previous day canning for Serena down at her house. "I'm near 'bout beaned out. And I wouldn't care if the beetles just took all the rest," muttered Iris as she adjusted the draft on the stove. Some summers Iris and Serena and Serena's cousin Rebecca would all work their beans, tomatoes, corn, or peaches together; sometimes just Iris and Serena would can together and put enough up for Rebecca, and sometimes Serena would not be able to get off work enough. Then Iris and Rebecca would work together, or they'd each work alone. During these times, Iris would try to put aside extra for Serena, since she knew her sister-in-law would be exhausted canning well after midnight and then having to get up early for work the next morning.

Soon Linda appeared at the screen door and, after a tentative knock, let herself in. "Well, look what the cat dragged," said Serena. "Where you been keeping yourself, honey?" Linda helped herself to the coffee, and pulling a chair up to the kitchen table, grabbed a handful of half runners.

Iris Buchanan was raised in Rocky Creek, although neither of her parents was from the community. Her mother came from Swope, a nearly deserted crossroads about ten miles away that had once been a booming railroad stop. The large boardinghouse and the Swope train station are abandoned now. As a young man in 1915, Iris's father had come from eastern North Carolina to the mountains, hoping to make his fortune in the then-booming timber industry. Iris's parents were married and settled in the large house at the foot of Rocky Creek near the school, the post office, and the country store.

When Iris was fifteen her father forbade her to go out alone with her beau and fellow musician, the twenty-four-year-old Harry Blackwelder. The year before, Iris's sixteen-year-old sister had eloped with a twenty-four year old man, and her father feared Iris would do the same. The next year Iris eloped with Harry's younger brother, J.B. After the initial tears and fears, all was forgiven and J.B. and Iris moved in with her parents. Iris's father liked J.B. and was glad she married a "mountain man." J.B.'s great grandfather had received a state land grant, and the Blackwelder family still retained a good amount of land in and around the community. Furthermore, J.B.'s father, John, had managed to expand his own holdings greatly through a profitable trucking business he had started, and J.B. had been working for his father since he was a young teenager.

Harry eventually moved to Ohio in search of work, married, and settled there. Iris and Harry are still close friends, and Iris and J.B. look forward to his several visits a year. Iris's parents remained in the community for only about a year after Iris had married J.B., and then they moved to Hayesville. The lumber industry was suffering decline in the county, and Iris's parents hoped to start over in the larger urban area.

Serena Wiseman was raised in a small-town environment and had some initial difficulty adapting to rural farm life when she married J.B.'s younger brother, Tom. Rocky Creek was not new to her, however, since she had cousins, aunts, and uncles in the community and had known Tom and the other Blackwelders well before marriage. Her parents had both grown up in the community; in fact, kin on the Wiseman side, as well as on her maternal grandmother Wilson's side, had been in the community at least since the early 1800s. Serena's father had been one of thirteen children and had left the community in search of work. Serena herself is one of eleven children who are now scattered from the mountains to the piedmont and north into Ohio. Serena's closest living relative still in the community is her father's sister, Estelle, who, with her husband from Hayesville, lives on 46 acres of the old Wiseman homeplace.

The Wisemans were at one time numerous in the hollow, but the name has all but disappeared. Flora Wiseman married Pontiac Jones, and the old couple owns 20 acres of the old Edd

Wiseman homeplace, as do Katherine Wiseman and her husband, Andrew, and W.W. Wiseman and his wife, Virginia. W.W. and Virginia own 114 acres and are the only remaining Wisemans in the community. The old Carolina Wiseman place, bought by John Blackwelder in the 1930s, is overgrown; only scant remains of an old chimney suggest past habitation. Thirty years' growth of pines cover the once-productive fields.

Linda and Larry Douthit bought their land from the estate of Maggie Wiseman Cook, whose husband and son had abandoned her after the Second World War to migrate north and had sold the house out from under her. Rebecca says that Maggie jokingly told her, "They didn't even invite me along." Maggie owned some of the old Edd Wiseman land, and with the help of relatives in the community, built the small, neatly stuccoed house where she lived alone for so many years. The flowers in bloom from early spring until the first frost confirm neighbors' appraisals of the character and disposition of the woman living alone in her little house tucked back in the woods.

Rebecca Wilson Phillips lives next door to her parents, Lonnie and Rachel Wilson, and alongside the land that her father had inherited from his parents. Ironically, Rebecca and her husband, Dale, rent part of the old Wilson homeplace that Fenton Hinkle, the lawyer in Brownsville, acquired from the Wilson family during an estate settlement. Although all of Rebecca's siblings moved away from the community, Rebecca has a number of Wilson cousins, aunts, and uncles in the community. Rebecca's husband, Dale, is a double relation to her, as Dale's father, who is Rebecca's father's first cousin, married his mother's first cousin. Dale and Rebecca had grown up together, and when Rebecca was sixteen and Dale was twenty-six they were married in a nearby state, with Rebecca's father witnessing the ceremony.

Dale's siblings all moved away from the community, although he has several aunts and uncles left nearby, and the Phillips name is fairly common in the community. Dale and Rebecca made moonshine until the risk began to outweigh the profits and have farmed since. Dale has worked in timber and the mines, and although he drinks heavily, for the past fifteen years he has held one of the few permanent blue-collar jobs with a local mining company. Rebecca makes quilts, grows broomcorn for her brooms, and farms with the eight of her ten children still left at home.

Dale's father, Charles, partially inherited and partially bought the two hundred acres on which Dale and his siblings grew up; Charles was born in the old log cabin near the new brick home that he built in the mid-1960s. Dale and Rebecca lived in the cabin for a while after they married, then rented Maggie's house until it was sold to the Douthits. Not long after the older couple moved into their new brick home, Charles's wife died, and Dale's unmarried sister, Elvira, who was working in Baltimore, gave up her urban job to care for her father and to help him farm his land.

Charles Phillips, who will gladly put down his labor to spend hours reminiscing about the past to any willing listener, said that he knew a man, now deceased, who was a distant relative of Frankie Silvers, famous in "the country" for having axed her man to death. In 1833, she became the first woman hanged in North Carolina.

Larry and Linda Douthit, first "hippies" and now neighbors, came up Rocky Creek in 1973. Others like them would follow. Initially viewed with curiosity akin to distaste, Larry and Linda gradually became real people, with their own shortcomings and gifts that would become, at some level, part of the structure of the community. As the favors and small kindnesses were extended between households, particularly from Iris and J.B. to the younger couple in need of so much, the ties between households emerged and grew stronger. Their needs were more basic than financial: they needed information, technology, basic tools, and strategies for coping with the everyday realities of mountain life, as well as with the occasional crisis of winter snow and frozen pipes, a car that sometimes would not run, and a road in constant need of repair. Sometimes resentful of the extent of their debt to J.B. and Iris, from whom they desperately tried to maintain some degree of autonomy and privacy, they nevertheless tried to reciprocate their obligations. As J.B. and Iris became more comprehensible to the younger couple, Linda and Larry became "some more of our young 'uns" to J.B. and Iris. They would never become totally one with the community, yet their place in Rocky Creek solidified with each passing season.

COMMUNITY

If early maps are taken as a guide, "community" was a cluster of dwellings, with a church, a school, a store, and a post office forming the center. A named place then, and still named on the map, community as it was then is a cluster of memories, historical relationships, and events for the old. An aunt remembers visiting the old store and the cluster of families who lived nearby; a former teacher taught in the community's school and lived in one of the nearby houses; a woman in her sixties grew up next door to the then-active post office and recalls the lively daily visiting.

In the 1980s, this center is no longer important. The school has long since closed; having survived use as a dwelling, it now stands vacant and is slowly being reclaimed by the woods surrounding it. The store, too, has closed; it also served as a dwelling for a time but now is going to ruin. The church still stands, well used by a small membership, though the parsonage was sold at public auction and moved, and other churches, nearby and distant, serve the spiritual needs of the community.

For the younger residents and newcomers, the community name now covers a wide area and is a series of roads flowing vaguely from one intersection to the next, rather than from ridge to ridge or from community to community. The twisting gravel road that wound along the hillsides above the fertile bottom land once carried travelers into and out of the community. But it was straightened, widened, and paved, so that travelers can speed along, in and out and through the community, never pausing, never noticing where the community begins and ends. In fact, only the old people know

where the boundaries are or were, when you're in Grassy Fork
or Lower Plum Tree or in Miller country; because only they
know with any certainty, the boundaries are no longer real or
important. Anyway, no Millers live in Miller country any-
more, and only one Woody lives on Woody Hill. And yet,
because the old folks know where it is, because the dead are
still buried next to their ancestors, because kinship ties still
weave neighbors into complicated networks of obligation and
recognition, and because neighbors still rely on each other for
friendship and mutual aid, community exists in the 1980s as
an important focus for each resident's life.

The community is in flux, particularly as family after
family has moved away, as old folks have died off, leaving the
homeplace to be sold, as outsiders in increasing numbers
have moved in and have no history there. Yet the community
has always been in flux; out-migration and out-marriage have
been part of community change since settlement. Families
and individuals have moved west, have gone off to war, have
sought their fortunes elsewhere, never to return home. Newcomers have married in, school teachers and government
agents have moved in and out, with some marrying in. Timber men, land speculators, teachers, and mineral speculators
have brought their families with them, and they or their
children have stayed to become part of the community.

As people have moved in, to stay for a few years or longer,
they have become part of the community. The events of their
lives have become interwoven with the rest of the community lore. Whether a teacher stayed and married, like Amanda
Miller did, to raise her children there or whether she left, her
time and experiences in the community are part of the local
history, social fabric, and lore. The back-to-the-landers who
arrived in 1970 or 1975 are a presence taken for granted by the
young, who have always known them. For other, older residents, they are viewed as outsiders at one level, yet their
interaction over the years has become part of the social fabric.
As outsiders have been involved in events, have shared the
changing seasons, local fears, frutrations, alarm, times of
mourning, and severe weather, or have been caught up in
family conflicts, they have been woven into the social fabric

and the local history. Whether or not they leave, their relationship to the community's history will not be forgotten or
denied.

Locally born families, back-to-the-landers, summer tourists, and nonnative retirees and other newcomers participate
in different social networks that serve a range of purposes and
carry with them a range of obligations. While these networks
are not tied to place, they come together in the place, in the
community. Community is a focus for overlapping networks
of interaction.

Community in the 1980s, like that in the 1880s, follows
the topography. It is the place between the ridges where
people live and where some make their living. The streams
are fed by springs on the mountainsides that provide water for
the homes and that course their way along the hillsides,
through the broad bottomland, and into the river down-
stream. Community is defined by geography and by the histories of the individuals who have lived there.

The boundaries of community in the 1980s are irrelevant.
Community as geography ends at the ridge, yet community
as interaction flows along the road, as the actions of individuals with each other and with institutions flow along the
roads.

Close relatives and newcomers share fencerows. Relatives
at odds with each other share the same kin and the same
roads. The poor and the not-so-poor live in proximity to each
other. While the poorer families traditionally lived high up
the hollows on less desirable land, the popularity of mountain summer homes with a view among nonnatives has resulted in a market for this less-productive land and in the
integration of fancier dwellings into the landscape. There are
no better-off or rough neighborhoods, streets, or sections.
Rich bottomland is commonly owned and worked by the
better-off family whose brick ranch-style or neatly painted
frame house is graced by an expansive, closely mowed lawn,
decorative shrubbery, and artfully placed flower beds. However, close by is the trailer on a corner of land or the dilapi-
dated rental house with sparse grass in the yard, the bodies of
vehicles that are temporarily out of use, or flowers in pots on

the porch or struggling against the assault of dogs, chickens, and children to bloom against the fence.

The flooding that morning in 1977 was yet one more event in the life of the community that brought neighbors into immediate helping and caring relationships with each other. As in any other major or minor disaster, unresolved hostilities were laid aside for a while as neighbors looked to neighbors for assistance and offered assistance in kind. These neighborhood associations lie below the surface during most of the year; they are irrelevant to most of the daily activities of the community during good times, normal times, when the business of working and just getting along consumes all the energy and time one can muster. Yet times of crisis and emergency bring these associations to the fore and provide the necessary energy to pull the neighborhood along, to reaffirm community, perhaps redefine for newer participants its underlying structure of mutual aid and communication.

Chapter Three

FAMILY, LAND, AND COMMUNITY

IN 1898 Amanda moved from the town of Jackson, where she was raised, into the Grassy Fork community to teach school. She married John Miller the next year. For the next forty years until her retirement, Amanda taught the children in the community, including her own eight children and one grandchild. Amanda and John's daughters Betty and Mary married Lewis brothers, and Amanda's own two brothers married two Lewis sisters. Amanda's daughter Mary, now an eighty-two-year-old widow, lives next to her daughter Sarah in a new trailer, put up to replace the old homeplace. Mary's mother-in-law, Lucy Woody, now a widow in her nineties, lives across the road, and three of her children live within sight of her house. Lucy's three brothers and their families live on up the road.

Down the other direction, Mary's daughter Evelyn lives with her husband and son, near Mary's brother's widow, Lynn. Next to Lynn is her son and his family. And so it goes around the community. Most households are connected by blood or by marriage, by close ties and distant, to other households in the community, and these kin ties form a basis for community life. With very few exceptions, families in the community are firmly rooted in extended and extensive networks of kin and in elaborate and often complicated communitywide kin relationships. As Mary noted about her own and her husband's kin relations in the community, "It's a mess. Maybe you can figure it all out."

Kinship and family in the rural mountain community are a highly valued and central part of life. Yet kinship is more than biological or genealogical connectedness; it is a cultural idea through which relationships are expressed and from which community homogeneity is derived. Kin ties connect commmunty residents into a system that gives personal identity through the expression of common roots, common ancestry, shared experience, and shared values; kinship also provides an idiom for people's behavior toward one another and is one of several bases for the actual formation of groups.

The child is born into a set of nurturing, sustaining relationships with a group of relatives. Throughout his or her life, parents, grandparents, siblings, aunts, uncles and cousins are interested in the individual's welfare and freely give love, support, and criticism. The individual matures into a social world in which family offers an atmosphere of trust, and the experiences of daily life give the individual no reason to doubt the constancy of family loyalty.

Glenda Wilson's dad went to Detroit with his brother in the 1920s in search of work. After several years her dad returned home to take up farming, an occupation that he and his son following him still pursue today. His brother stayed in Detroit, and over the years, as correspondence diminished, the family gradually lost track of him. However, contact with the long-lost brother was reestablished during the 1960s; the old uncle, alone and in poor health, was brought back home to live out his last days among his kin. "Nobody had seen him for forty years, but when they brought him home it was like it had been a day." Glenda continues, "Folks around here are that way, they'll take in their black sheep, their wanderers, 'cause they're family, no matter what."

Land and family, place and kinship are intimately interwoven and value laden. Historically, as Eller has written,

Land held a special meaning that combined the diverse concepts of utility and stewardship. While land was something to be used and developed to meet one's needs, it was also the foundation of daily existence giving form to personal identity, material culture, and economic life. As such, it defined the "place" in which one found security and self-worth. Family, on the other hand, as the central organizing unit of social life, brought substance and order to that sense of place. Strong family ties influenced almost every aspect of the social system, from the primary emphasis upon informal personal relationships to the pervasive egalitarian spirit of local affairs. Familism, rather than the accumulation of material wealth, was the predominant cultural value in the region, and it sustained a lifestyle that was simple, methodical, and tranquil. [1982:38]

Kinship is a cultural value, connecting the individual to other people, to land, to community, to history, and to identity. The "Decoration Day" services, commonly at churches or family cemeteries in many mountain communities, provide a time for recognition and celebration of this continuity of family and place through time. On Decoration Day, descendants of persons buried in family cemeteries congregate to honor the dead and to renew old relationships.

In the Rocky Creek community, Decoration Day is held on one Sunday each year. In addition, because of the overlapping nature of kin ties in the community, it is celebrated on different Sundays for each of the six family cemeteries. Because of the complex, kin-group intermarriages, especially in the past, and thus the overlapping kinship ties connecting members of the community to each other, an individual may have ancestors buried in several of the family cemeteries. Thus one may acknowledge status in several different categories of people who have common ancestry. Consequently, some individuals celebrate several different Decoration Days.

Traditionally, the eldest male of the family, as head of the extended family group, would go with a grandson to the cemetery on the eve of Decoration Day to clean up, cut the grass, and trim around the stones and along the fence surrounding the cemetery. On Decoration Day morning, relatives convene at the cemetery and cover the graves with freshly cut flowers. Prayers are offered by older men of the assembled families; scripture reading and preaching may take place if someone is so moved. The most rewarding activity for most people, who may drive quite a distance to attend these events is the renewing of old acquaintances and the sharing of family gossip. For many, this is the only chance during the year to see out-of-community relatives, even those living close by. In one family, for example, two brothers who lived within fifty miles of each other saw each other only once each year, at this festivity. After spending several hours in the cemetery, family members congregate at the house of the eldest resident family member for a covered-dish dinner. About mid to late afternoon the group breaks up, everyone goes home, and ancestry is put aside for another year.

Decoration Day can also be a time of healing, of mending old wounds between family members. Iris wondered one Sunday morning, "How can I face my mother's grave?" Tensions were running high that morning because of conflicts with her husband's brother and sister-in-law and their children, who lived next door, latent during most of the year but rekindled and stirred by the barrage of visiting relatives from Ohio. Yet face them she did, and the tears that streamed down her face as she embraced her kinfolk in the cemetery sprang from a wealth of emotions: hostility, guilt, anger, and love.

THE KINSHIP IDIOM

Each person is born into a set of kinship relationships—a kindred, a network of individuals. These ties provide a variety of potential relationships that the individual can use when the need arises. Kinship ties thus provide a basis for reciprocal exchange, assistance, and the formation of groups; but kinship also provides an idiom for the way in which people *should* behave toward each other.

When Linda and Larry Douthit moved into Rocky Creek in 1970 they knew no one in the area. J.B. and Iris Blackwelder helped them out in many ways—both in getting them settled in their house and in beginning their farming activities. When Larry's mother, an upper-middle-class urban woman who disapproved heartily of her son's lifestyle, arrived unexpectedly, Iris took a freshly baked cake over to the house so that Linda and Larry would have some refreshments. Linda and Larry feel some strain in the relationship with the Black-welders because they do not have the means to reciprocate the many favors done for them. They try, however, to do whatever they can to help Iris and J.B. On occasion, Linda has done some bookkeeping for the Blackwelder trucking firm and has helped Iris with canning and freezing. Sometimes Larry helps J.B. in his farming. At other times he drives J.B., who periodically has vision difficulties, to places he needs to go. Linda and Larry have been incorporated into Iris and J.B.'s set of socially important kin and are sometimes referred to as "some more of our young 'uns." Likewise, Larry half-jokingly refers to J.B. as "Uncle J.B."

Women who become close friends through mutual visiting and mutual exchange may refer to each other as being "like a sister to me," and women may refer to their mother's close friends as having been "like a second mother to me." Friends may be incorporated into socially important relationships through the idiom of kinship, specifically through the use of fictive kinship terms. For example, Maxine and Cecil developed a close visiting relationship with the young couple who rented their house. On one occasion, at a large gathering at the high school, Maxine introduced the young renters to her friends as "some more of our young 'uns."

Use of the terms "aunt" and "uncle" is a common means of incorporating people into socially important groups through fictive kinship. These terms are used in respect for older people with whom one has developed socially important ties. Just as Larry refers to the older man as "Uncle J.B.," J.B. refers to his older cousin as "Uncle Jason," the old man Charles Phillips refers to the long-deceased, nonkin woman from whom his father bought his land as "Aunt Jane Wilson," and old John Blackwelder refers to a now-deceased, nonkin neighbor as "Uncle Scott Weldon." These terms of address are thus used to incorporate both kin and nonkin into close kin categories.

Socially important relationships are expressed in terms of an "idiom of kinship." There are certain expected or ideal patterns of reciprocal activity and mutual aid between close kin; kinship provides a prototype for ideal social relationships. The idiom of kinship dominates most social relationships in the community.

To be surrounded by an extensive network of kin, an extended family, is an ideal. Parents want the best for their children and recognize that, to a greater or lesser extent, their children at some point must be on their own and make their own way. If that means leaving the community or even leaving the mountains, then parents can accept it. Yet, to have children and grandchildren close at hand is a fine and highly desirable state of affairs.

When several generations of a family are able to live in the community—when married children can find work close enough at hand to reside locally and when land can be spared or acquired for a house or a mobile home—then families can be residentially clustered near each other. While married children establish a separate household as soon as possible, usually upon marriage, a common pattern for children who can find the means to live locally is for parents who have land to provide them with an acre or two. Because of the high cost of new homes and the scarcity of rental housing, children quite often put up a mobile home on their parents' land.

When such family clusters do occur, extended-family activity groups are the natural result. Cooperation among related families is useful in gardening, farming, building, equipment use and repair, food storage, and a range of other activities. Through their cooperative efforts and residential patterns, the image of a solidary, unified family group is established. Efforts to mobilize and unify the separate nuclear families rest with the older generation, the parents, who have authority by virtue of age, experience, and ownership of property and equipment.

OTHER GROUPS

Members of different nuclear families come together for economic, social, and ritual purposes. Most commonly, people come together in seasonal work groups for agricultural work such as setting out and working tobacco, putting up hay, clearing land, putting up food for winter storage, or harvesting cash crops such as beans, cabbages, or tomatoes. These "activity groups" may or may not be composed of close kin, or even solely of kin; their composition changes often, depending on the activity. Individuals and families may have multiple ties and obligations throughout the community and will work and socialize with different individuals and families at different times and for different purposes throughout the year.

Seasonal work groups usually come together for agricultural work. Close kin who also live near each other commonly share such work, and if extra labor is needed, a close kinsman who lives outside the community may also come to help. Rachel, her sister Ruth, and Rachel's daughter Rebecca frequently work together in farming, harvesting, and food storage and simply enjoy visiting together as well. They are sometimes joined by Amy, also a neighbor, the wife of Rachel's husband's cousin. Rachel, Rebecca, and Ruth gave a wedding shower for Rebecca's son Fred. Rebecca and Ruth make quilts and sew together. The relationship among the three women is one of warmth and great mutual confidence.

Neighbor children will occasionally be hired to help in seasonal work. A residentially close, nonkin neighbor may also join in the work, and the labor will be reciprocated at another time. A man with a harvester may harvest several neighbors' fields, and the neighbors will help him harvest his own and put up his tobacco. A good mechanic will repair a neighbor's car or help pull an engine, and the neighbors will help the mechanic reroof his house.

Andy sought Fred Miller's help on several occasions, since Fred and his son Fred Junior have the equipment, expertise, and spare parts to pull and replace an automobile engine, rebuild a carburetor, or weld a lawn-mower handle back together. When Fred cut his hay, he called on Andy to help, and Andy spent three evenings working with Fred, Fred's wife, Geneva, a neighbor boy, and Fred's cousin. Andy also helped Fred put the roof on Fred's new barn. Andy couldn't anticipate when Fred would call on him, but he had no doubt about his obligation and dropped everything he was doing when Fred called for help with the hay. Andy says, "Fred put down everything he was doing when I needed his help and spent most of the morning helping me with that old engine."

Male kinsmen sometimes come together for ongoing economic enterprises, and the cooperative labor provides support for each household. John Blackwelder is the father of Tom, Walton, J.B., and Johnny and the grandfather of Billy, Mark, Steve, and Bob, all of whom are involved to different degrees in a family trucking business that was built by John. Managerial responsibility has passed from John to his son J.B. and to J.B.'s son Mark, while Tom owns several of the trucks and makes most of his business contracts independently of those made by Mark. Tom's two sons, Steve and Bob, usually work for their father, although they occasionally drive for Mark. Grandson Billy is primarily a mechanic and works in J.B.'s garage, both on the family trucks and on jobs that he has contracted independently.

Participation in such work groups is primarily influenced by kinship. Close kin—including lineal relatives (parents, grandparents, great-grandparents, and their children) and their spouses; siblings, their children, and spouses; parents' siblings and their children; spouse and spouse's close kin—are those to whom obligatins are felt and on whom one can call for help. A second factor influencing group participation is residence in the community. Nonkin neighbors may help each other before nonresident kinfolks, particularly when nonkin neighbors are also friends. A third factor is the economic obligation one may have to reciprocate past or anticipated help to a neighbor, as well as the need for help from neighbors.

Several factors may preclude participation in community groups, including public-work obligations, although neighbors will quite often pitch in and help with whatever labor is going on after they get off work. Hostilities or quarrels among close kin may also preclude sharing labor; two brothers or two sisters-in-law may adamantly avoid working together in an otherwise family work group because of an ongoing quarrel.

LAND AND FAMILY

Land is the most valuable resource for the rural community and thus the most controversial object of inheritance. Furthermore, the ideal of the independent nuclear family places a high value on individual property ownership as an added assurance of continuing family independence and as a symbol of financial security. Yet, parents need the help of married children and their families in working the land and also desire to keep children "in the fold," loyal to the family. Likewise, young couples need the help of others because they have not raised a labor force of children and do not always have access to capital for hiring labor or purchasing equipment. Parents, who are often in control of resources, may therefore manipulate potential ownership of land by children in order to assure their children's loyalty and cooperation in collective activities.

A newly married couple's decision to stay in the community after marriage is primarily affected by three factors: the availability of adequate housing, the probability that they will inherit or be able to buy land, and the availability of work. Because of these three factors, many young people leave the community either to reside in another nearby community or to migrate out of the region altogether. In particular, many young people leave the community to find work, recognizing that the prospects are dim for making a living in a rural community with limited job and land possibilities.

Land is most frequently obtained from older family members, often through inheritance. Inheritance ideally involves an equal distribution of property among all children, regardless of age, sex, or other considerations. Such inheritance is, however, an ideal. Eighty-six-year-old Charles Phillips said that, when he was first married, he told his wife: "Now, I want us to live right and raise six children, and I want us to manage to work out six hundred acres of land, give 'em a hundred acres apiece, and build 'em all a good nice home." The reality of their situation deflated his ideal, however, when his wife cut him off with, "Let the God-durned young 'uns work just like we worked."

In a few cases, in spite of dwindling holdings, the ideal of equal inheritance by all children has prevailed, with predictable results. For example, one of the better Rocky Creek farms—one with fertile, flat land and ample water—had lain vacant for a number of years since the death of the owners. The eleven children of the deceased couple inherited equal shares of the 155-acre farm but could not decide on the disposition of the property. On this land stands a 150-year-old cabin; in it, five generations of the family have grown up. Yet, because several of the heirs wanted to farm the land, while several wanted to develop it for real estate purposes, people in the community suspected that the entire farm would be sold to the highest bidder, and the money divided equally. The highest bidder would, no doubt, have been a developer, as none of the farming children (or any of the local farmers) had enough money to purchase the land. The problem was partially resolved when the land was surveyed and divided into eleven equal shares, and the children drew to determine who received which share. Whether one or more of the heirs would be able to buy out the others remained to be seen.

Before the mid-1960s each child's inheritance of some portion of the family estate created no overwhelming difficulties in Rocky Creek. Even though inherited landholdings might be small, the possibilities usually existed for consolidating landholdings through marriage or for expanding holdings through purchase. In addition, although the amount of readily usable (that is, cleared) land was in fact limited, it was and still is, possible to clear forested land. Depopulation of the rural communities since the 1960s and the decline of agriculture have meant that much hillside land that was actively farmed by earlier generations has been allowed to revert to timber. Although sections of the forested land in the community are too severe and rocky for agriculture or pasturage, some forested plots are cultivable.

Several factors may alter the principle of equal inheritance and/or affect the acquisition of land by local families. First, the youngest child is expected to remain closer to the parents than other siblings and to take care of any needs that may arise. Adherence to this practice depends on the age and physical condition of the parents. Thus if the parents are old or unable to assume major responsibilities at the time the youngest child marries or departs from home, parents and older siblings will tend to expect the youngest child, more than any of the others, to remain close to the parents. It is usual for the youngest child who stays close to the parents to inherit more property than his or her siblings. Throughout the mountain area, the "baby" occupies a special position in the family. Yet, at least one person mentioned that the youngest child in a family may be more likely to leave the area altogether, because family responsibilities and expectations, sibling pressures, and threatened loss of independence can become quite overwhelming.

Second, in families in which sons are involved in working the land with their fathers, parents will sometimes deed or sell a greater portion of land to sons than to daughters. The male work patterns established in a family sometimes continue after the son marries. Consequently, if a cooperative economic venture is occupationally feasible for a family group and if, as a result, a married son and his family remain residentially close to the son's parents, the son is apt to receive a greater portion of land than siblings, male or female, who have moved away. In such cases, parents often attempt to compensate other siblings financially. This practice is not limited to the farming family; the Blackwelder family trucking concern has supported six nuclear families in various capacities. Residential decisions are occasionally influenced by the desire to continue male work units in large-scale economic activities. As a result, families tend to live closer to the husband's parents than to the wife's.

A third factor affecting land acquisition is out-migration. The lure of fortunes to be made in the northern industrial centers, western timber, Kentucky coal, and elsewhere, as well as the lack of work locally, drew many potential inheritors of family property permanently away from the community. The siblings left behind thus received larger shares of the family property. In several families, children inherited land only if they remained in the community; in others, inheritors of family property who left the community sold their portions of the family holdings to siblings left behind, at reasonable rates. Out-migration remains significant in the community, although sale of land to siblings has been greatly affected by the development of a full-scale recreation industry since the 1960s, the popularity of second homes in the mountains, and the resulting rapidly increasing cost of land. For the young family with no equity and only a minimal income, the possibility of purchasing land in the communities in which they grew up is becoming increasingly remote. In two decades, the cost of farmland has jumped from between two hundred and four hundred dollars per acre to well over one thousand dollars an acre, and even hillside land prices have skyrocketed. While large acreage (eighty acres or more) can still be obtained for as little as five hundred dollars an acre or sometimes less, young families and those who want to farm are usually priced out of the market. With the increasing value of farmland have come increasing taxes and increasing land sale by farmers.

> Agriculture, especially at the small scale common (in western North Carolina), often does not generate the income necessary to pay these taxes and farmers feel compelled to sell all or part of their land or to abandon agriculture as an occupation and seek employment in other sectors. . . . Just as it is difficult to maintain a farm, it is even more difficult to begin a career in farming. As land prices rise with speculation, young persons wishing to go into farming are priced out of the market for land. As a result, farming has become less of an alternative as both an occupation and lifestyle, and is increasingly maintained by older, well-established farmers. [Appalachian Land Ownership Task Force, 1981:26]

A fourth factor affecting land acquisition is the recent increase in land sale to outsiders. Many people who live in the community consider themselves "land poor" and recognize that the only way to make money off land, particularly land unsuitable for farming or grazing, is to sell it to developers, land speculators, summer people, or outsiders moving in. Consequently, those who remain in the community and wish to buy land for farming often cannot afford to pay the price that outsiders, and particularly land speculators, are able to offer. Individuals who decide to remain in the community have little assurance that kinsmen will sell land to them at prices they can afford.

While most of the rural land in western North Carolina communities is privately owned, an increasing number of owners are nonlocal, and the number of local residents owning large tracts of land is declining. Although an increasing number of nonlocal people are buying land for second-home development or for speculation, corporate interests, including timber, land development, and mining corporations, also control a considerable amount of local land.

Population pressure on the land has not been a factor in ownership or division of farms, since out-migration from rural communities has been occurring since World War II. While out-migration from the region slowed during the 1960s, migration from rural areas to towns continued through the 1970s.

The economic base of rural mountain communities has not been altered significantly with the increase in tourism, particularly in those communities located far from the resort areas of the counties, although the tourism industry has created an inflationary economic situation. Thus many families who, fifteen or twenty years ago, would have been in a position to expand their landholdings, are now trapped in a situation in which the potential for expansion is dismal, while others cannot afford to keep what they have.

Parents, who own the major portion of available land and either do not have children in the household or realistically anticipate the loss of children from the household, need the help of married children and their families in working the land. Parents are therefore reluctant to deed children their share of the inheritance immediately upon marriage, for this would result not only in the splitting up of the larger land unit and the loss of assurance that the products of the deeded land will benefit the parents but also in the threat of losing the labor of the younger family unit and the control over this labor pool, which would represent a threat to the solidarity of the extended family. One way of ensuring family cooperation is for parents to deed or, occasionally, to sell to children a small plot of land on which to build their own houses. Children thus own their own land and help work the parents' land, with the expectation that they will inherit a larger portion of the land than siblings who live farther away. Historically, land was sold to children before there was any significant land pressure. In a family history of one of the earliest families to settle in Rocky Creek, it is recorded that "beginning about 1823, 'broken down' and unable to walk due to 'the rheumatiz' or arthritis, [X] began selling his lands to his children for nominal sums which he used for maintenance of himself and [his wife]." Four different sons were sold 312, 246, 150, and 82 acres, and two sons-in-law were sold 206 and 200 acres. The "homeplace," of undetermined acreage, was given to the youngest son. One of the sons later sold his land to a third sister's husband when the son moved away from the community. After the first passage to the youngest son, the family homeplace was not passed to other youngest children, although it "remained in the hands of [X's] descendants for more than a hundred years after his death, which occurred in 1833 or 34." The present owner of the twelve remaining acres of the eighty-two acre plot is a great-great-grandson of the original owner.

Land, the most valuable resource in the community, is the most controversial object of inheritance. The principle of independence of the family of marriage from extended-family obligations and controls reinforces a high value on individual property ownership. Furthermore, the conflict between nuclear-family independence and the necessity for extended-family economic cooperation creates a structural bind. Each nuclear family desires independent landownership. Parents desire cooperation from married children and their families. Parents are in the position to hold land as incentive for the young family to contribute to the solidary, extended-family cooperative unit.

The case of Charles Phillips, who wanted to give each child one hundred acres, reflects this problem. Charles's unmarried daughter has lived with him since the death of his wife, taking care of all the domestic duties and farming. Charles had one married son in the community, Dale Phillips, who had seven children living at home. Dale Phillips and his wife, Rebecca, who owned no land, were renting. Dale and Rebecca had lived with Charles for several years after they married but eventually moved away, into a house next to Rebecca's parents, primarily because Charles and Rebecca could not get along.

In the early fall of 1973, Dale, Rebecca, and the children bought a new mobile home and did move back to the father's land. While fearing the problems that would arise from living near and working with her domineering old father-in-law, Rebecca was eager to have a home of her own. Dale and Rebecca wanted Charles to give them their inheritance, but Charles resisted this idea and was highly resentful of the suggestion by some of his other children, who didn't live nearby, that he make a will.

The move of Dale's family back to his father's land was probably encouraged by the fact that Charles had sold several large tracts of land to outsiders and that he had had a number of good offers for the rest of his land by a local developer (who, incidentally, talked the old man out of making a will when Charles asked him to draw one up). Charles did deed to Dale one acre (out of his 126) when the move was made. Charles considers himself "land poor"—that is, owning land that is not productive without the help of a number of people and worth money only when sold. Moreover, two of Dale and Rebecca's children were working in factory jobs but were unmarried and still living at home, thus contributing both capital and some farm labor to the family. These children were expected to contribute to the cost of the new trailer as long as they remained in residence.

To summarize, Charles wanted to keep his land, continue farming, and have good workers under his thumb, without giving them the freedom that would result from his giving them the land. Dale's family owned only one acre, they wanted to farm and maintain a comfortable, "traditional," independent existence, but they had to satisfy Charles's desires in order to receive a possible share of the inheritance (before the speculator did). They now maintain two separate residences approximately fifty yards apart, and Charles, his daughter Elvira, Rebecca, the younger children when they are not in school, and the older children when they are not at work farm the land together. On the other hand, Fred Miller is one of the largest landowners in Grassy Fork, yet he leases his son the land upon which Fred Junior has built his house and garage.

In the case of the Blackwelders, J.B. and Iris lived with Iris's parents upon marriage and then "were given" five acres by J.B.'s parents, on which they built their house. Similarly, another son and his wife were given seven acres of land. They say that, although the land was given to them, they have paid for it many times over. The problem of land distribution in this particular extended family is more complicated and deserves some attention.

John Blackwelder, patriarch of the extended family, grew up on a farm just outside the community. He married Lisa Profitt, who grew up in the community on a farm now owned by Lisa's nephew. Lisa's father gave John and Lisa a few acres of land and helped them build the house in which John and his second wife, Louise, still live. After several years of marriage, John and Lisa bought approximately 390 acres of land (194 of which John still owns) adjacent to the land on which they were living. Several years later Lisa died, and as the house was in her name, Lisa willed it to her children.

John remarried and had three more children. He persuaded the six children by his first marriage to deed him the house, and he in turn agreed to deed to them 200 acres of land he had bought, an agreement that was never put in writing. In 1969, however, John's grandson-in-law Joe, who lives in Burnsville, talked John into selling him approximately 150 acres of the land in question at a low price and the money from this sale was distributed equally among the six children. Joe then resold the land to another man outside the community at a twenty-thousand-dollar profit to himself. In 1973 John sold another 40 acres of the land for twelve thousand dollars to a land speculator outside the community. John says that he sold the land because he is old and poor and needs the money. The six children feel that they have been cheated of their inheritance because, first, they were not consulted on the matter and would never have allowed it to go for such a pittance; second, they had no intentions of letting the land go anyway; and third, they say that John is by no means poor. Two of the first six children, J.B. and Tom, live on small plots clustered near John, on land that he gave them. As I noted earlier, one son lives just outside the community on John's homeplace, which he inherited from John's brother, and the three remaining children live outside the state. Two of these three had planned to build retirement homes on their share of the land, and all resent the "swindle." The resentment is directed toward John and toward Joe, who is considered quite a wheeler-dealer. The resentment is controlled, however, as no one feels he has the right to interfere; on the surface, relations among the parties involved are quite amicable.

In sum, there is an ideal of equal inheritance, by all children of family property, yet, in practice two factors work against this ideal. First, land prices are inflated with respect to local economic potential. Because of high prices, one's potential inheritance may be sold to people outside the family or community and potential inheritors may be forced to leave the area and thus forfeit their inheritance. Second, inheritance is one element that may, on occasion, be manipulated by those in control of resources in order to ensure the cooperation of the residentially close but supposedly independent families of children. Extended-family cooperation ensures an economic margin of security to cooperating family units, in spite of the primary self-sufficiency of each nuclear family.

SOLIDARITY AND CONFLICT

The nuclear family is supposed to have an element of autonomy or independence from parents and parents-in-law, yet extended families are supposed to act like family, that is, to share resources, labor, time, and love. While newlyweds have come from families expecting family loyalty, the adjustment to the requirements of loyalty and cooperation with a new spouse's family may be difficult to make.

The subtle, and sometimes not so subtle, tensions that arise from family pressures from both the older and younger couple's points of view are dealt with in a variety of ways. Frustration and annoyance are vented through gossip; mounting tensions or continuing, irreconcilable differences are dealt with by avoidance; and occasionally, continuing and mounting hostilities can be dealt with through threats or acts of violence.

If a newly married couple stays in the community, they usually reside in a separate house or trailer close to the parents of one or the other. When the couple settles near the husband's parents, the husband and his male kinsmen continue working together in those agricultural activities requiring cooperative labor or, in some cases, in joint business ventures. The products of the collective labor benefit each separate household. The new wife is expected to merge into the female work unit and to contribute her energy to her new family group. If a couple settles near the wife's parents, the same is expected. The new husband should merge into the male work unit, and the wife should contribute her labor to the female work unit.

If both sets of parents live in the community or if one set lives in the community and the other nearby, the couple may have double obligations and expectations. Friction may arise over the distribution of the new couple's labor and over the expectations of visiting. The promise of land, as well as closer proximity, may reinforce a couple's affiliation with one particular set of kin. However, the more distant parents may pressure the couple to continue in established patterns of visiting and even work sharing.

Hazel and Bob and their seven children live on land given to them by Bob's parents, who live about one-quarter mile away. Bob's job keeps him away from home most of the time, and the burden of family obligation falls squarely on Hazel's shoulders. Maxine and Cecil, Bob's parents, rarely find anything kind to say about Hazel, complaining that Hazel "can throw more out the back door with a teaspoon than her husband can bring in the front door with a shovel." Hazel, who has no relatives nearby, says that her parents-in-law resent the fact that she and the children won't be controlled in the way that Bob has always been controlled. Hazel in turn complains of Bob's overattention to his parents' needs and his neglect of his own family. Hazel copes with an uncomfortable existence by gossip and, as much as possible, by avoidance. While she and the children must help with the family farm work, she says that she doesn't have much to say to her parents-in-law, because whatever she says they'll criticize. Maxine refers to Hazel as "that old slab-sided thing," and Hazel refers to "*my* mother-in-law, the stubborn old coot."

Women have also dealt with such family frustrations by running away. Running away usually meant returning to the woman's natal household; several women laughingly told of doing this as young brides. One woman, whose parents did not live in the community but whose ancestors for five generations had done so and who had several aunts and uncles nearby, "ran away" on four or five different occasions, as she simply could no longer tolerate her parents-in-law's demands on her labor. She would walk down to the tracks, flag down the passenger train, and travel to her parents' home, about thirty miles away. She likewise told of getting her brothers to lie for her, to tell her husband she was ill so that she wouldn't have to return to him or to say that other family members were ill so that she would have an excuse for being home. On each of these occasions, either her husband would come after her or her parents would insist that she return on her own. As in other such cases, a woman's parents would usually receive her for a short period, but since the attitude is overwhelmingly that nuclear families should stay together if possible, she would be encouraged to return to her husband.

Relationships among unrelated women who marry into the same family may contain an element of strain or potential conflict; in such a case, contacts are usually simply avoided. Thus two women who married brothers each told of conflict with their sister-in-law, brother-in-law, and parents-in-law. Although two sisters-in-law now live next door to each other whose husbands usually work together, neither has visited the other or has been in the other's house for a number of years. Furthermore, one of the women refuses to attend social gatherings, such as family dinners, at the nearby house of parents-in-law. She states that there is always conflict, normally in the form of criticism of her children's behavior, and she simply refuses to tolerate it any more.

Men who are feeling the pressure of being the less-than-perfect or perhaps unsatisfactory in-married spouse occasionally confide in a close, nonaffine friend. One young man complained bitterly to such a friend of the hostility he felt toward his wife's parents, who lived next door and who partially supported his family of three. This man was expected to help his father-in-law with farming, but he resented the control that the older couple had over his family. He eventually left his wife and baby, although whether the separation will be permanent is yet unknown.

Husbands occasionally confide in a sympathetic older child. Furthermore, many middle-aged men in the community work during the week away from the community and therefore have means for venting their feelings away from the domestic scene that are not as available for the older generation of women. Younger and middle-aged women, who are largely employed in local mills, also have the workplace in which to vent frustrations and find support.

The parents-in-law of one man refer to their son-in-law as "that drunken, lazy, good-for-nothing sot" and say that they cannot understand how their daughter could possibly stay married to him. A daughter-in-law of the same parents, who gets along equally poorly with them, says that they offered their daughter money to leave her husband (although the validity of this statement is questionable). Although the son-in-law never complained much, he did have a tendency to go "out with the boys" and to get drunk rather frequently; it was suggested by his in-married sister-in-law that, whenever the parents criticized him for being a "drunken sot," he would get drunk, which would increase their criticism.

As mentioned above, men and women have somewhat different means of dealing with strain, due to different socialization and roles in the system. Violence is an alternative rarely used by either sex, but in the past there had been several cases of men using violence as a means of dealing with overwhelming and increasing expectations and criticism. In one such instance in the 1950s, a couple attended a gathering at one of the two churches in the community, to which the wife's parents came as well. The parents had been attempting to interfere with the couple since they were married and continued to heap abuse on the husband's activities during the social. He left the church and walked the mile up the mountain to his home for his gun, returned to the church, shot his father-in-law and brother-in-law as they emerged from the church, and after he had chased her around the church, finally succeeded in shooting his mother-in-law. He then drove himself to the sheriff's office and turned himself in. This man was released from prison on good behavior after serving seven years and returned to the community, where he was accepted back as a neighbor (although not necessarily one to cross). His wife had divorced him, so he married the widow of his mother's deceased brother, a person in a much safer relationship to him.

In the perspective of the extended family, there are several cases of violence against those who threaten the solidarity of the kin group. In one such case, an outsider to a large extended-family group that was clustered nearby in a single, relatively isolated hollow started courting one of the daughters of the family. In addition, he began to socialize with several of the daughter's brothers. Together, these young men frequently spent time drinking and driving, getting into fights and whatever trouble they could find. One evening the patriarch of the family, an excellent marksman, waited on the side of the mountain and, as the car full of young men rode by, shot and killed the potential affine, thereby eliminating the threat of future disruption to his group. In a recent case, the drunken father and leader of an extended family attempted to push his daughter and son-in-law's mobile home off the side of the mountain, when no one was inside. The restraint that had existed in the tension between the two men had been broken down by alcohol (which perhaps explains the father-in-law's attempting the push with a Volkswagen Beetle—he failed.)

For men and women there are basically three alternative solutions to potential conflict. The first is violence, but the consequences of such action are severe and therefore restrictive, whether enforced by law or by community opinion. Furthermore, violence is a dramatic type of interference with another person's life and is ultimately a break in the code of noninterference. Violence most often is preceded by threats of violence, which normally are heeded, so that a second solution—avoidance—is more often followed. In some cases, however, individuals believe that their own independence and therefore their worth has been so damaged or threatened that it can be regained to a degree only through violent destruction of the cause.

Religious ritual is a third, but rarely heeded, strategy. Decoration Day provides a ceremony through which individuals may on occasion seek resolution of difficulties. The frequent spontaneous preaching by members of the group is one means of easing hostilities that may exist between those preaching and other family members. As one person noted, Decoration Day is a time for "clearing the air," so that "if you've done something against somebody and you let it out with the help of the Lord, and ask his help and intervention in public, then nobody can say 'that son-of-a-bitch.'" Decoration Day in some ways serves the function of settling, or at least easing, potential hostilities.

In the face of hostilities, then, avoidance is a solution and God is the only mediator. But where avoidance is not possible and God doesn't listen, then violent action is a logical alternative.

The independent nuclear family is an ideal state of existence, since extended-family cooperation enhances the economic status of all families involved. Independent ownership of land by nuclear families is greatly valued. Land is, however, usually acquired from parents. Parents and married children each need the other's resources, since parents often have land and equipment but need labor and since children often can supply labor but have limited financial resources, land, and equipment. Parents are therefore in a position to influence their married children's lives. Inheritance is one factor that can be manipulated by those in control of resources in order to ensure the cooperation of the residentially close but ideally independent families of children. Affinal strain thus results from the conflict between the ideal independence of nuclear families and the necessity for subordination of nuclear-family interests to those of parents. This strain specifically occurs between in-married spouses and their parents-in-law.

A final qualification must be added: this system, like all rural social systems, is changing. With the decreasing viability of agriculture and the increasing reliance on "public work," as well as the increasing number of occupational and educational possibilities that are becoming real alternatives to the mountain young person, the necessity for extended-family cooperation is decreasing. Affinal strain is becoming increasingly uncommon and, for those who do not choose to leave the community altogether, is more easily handled by simple avoidance when it does occur. Furthermore, as illustrated by a 1973 case of multiple murder in a nearby community, in which the son-in-law killed not only his parents-in-law but also his wife and himself, a violent solution to a problem now represents a case of absolute desperation when no possible alternatives exist.

Chapter Four

SEX ROLES AND THE LIFE CYCLE

THE NEW BABY finally arrived after a day and a half in coming. Frances and Andy had waited until the contractions were three minutes apart, then they called Frances's mother to let her know they were on their way and headed for the hospital, twenty-five miles away. They were both excited, nervous, and a little frightened. Andy took the unpaved shortcut over the hill amid Frances's protests: "Go easy over these bumps, Andy. Why in the hell are we going this way anyway? We've got plenty of time . . . I hope."

Frances worked long and hard through the next day and well into the second night before Elizabeth finally struggled into the world. Andy waited outside, kept company by Frances's mother and other relatives who dropped by during the day and early evening. Elizabeth (named after a grandmother and a great-grandmother) was their first child, a beautiful, healthy, nine-pound girl. Andy called to her through the nursery window, and in the early hours after midnight, they let him hold her for a while. At first he was afraid to hold her, she was so tiny and seemed so fragile, but she slept peacefully in his arms as he talked softly to her and to her mother.

Though she hadn't put too much store in it, two different neighbor women had told Frances to be ready on the new moon; sure enough, the maternity ward had been overflowing that night, with Frances and Andy among the expectant parents. Several women had predicted its sex by the way Frances carried the baby, though there was some disagreement on the interpretation. About half the predictions were wrong.

Once when Frances was working in the garden, a black snake slithered across her path. Her aunt was quite alarmed that the baby would be marked, and she recalled children whose birthmarks, personalities, or health had been shaped by their mothers' prenatal experiences and activities. A mother who craves strawberries, for example, might bear a child with a strawberry-shaped birthmark. Consequently, exposure to death and illness were to be avoided.

In the hospital Frances had tried not to be distracted or alarmed during her labor by the younger girl down the hall, whose screams and moans of mingled fear and pain had echoed through the labor area for a time during the evening. The young girl had not seen a doctor before that night and had not expected the baby so soon; her unemployed, uninsured, and equally frightened young husband waited alone outside. The nursing staff had worked closely and gently with the young girl, and well before Elizabeth was born, this exhausted mother rested quietly and comfortably, cooing at the tiny infant in her arms. The nursing staff encouraged bonding of mother and child by urging the new mother to hold the child as soon as it was born and then by giving mother and child time together in the labor room after the baby had been examined by the pediatrician and had been dressed.

Husband-assisted childbirth, though neither unheard of nor frowned upon, is rather a rarity in the rural community. Although local doctors and the local hospital, adapting to the desires of the nursing staffs and urbanized town population, encourage prepared childbirth classes and husband involvement, childbirth for the rural population remains primarily the domain of women. Family members join the expectant father to wait together away from the delivery area, getting their first glimpse of the new relative through the nursery window.

The next morning Frances and Elizabeth were visited by neighbors—not by those who had driven the twenty-five miles to the hospital for a too-early call but by those who worked there, who carpooled in every weekday morning. The three neighbor women whose shifts began at 7:00 A.M. left home at 6:00 to meet at the store, shift cars, then pick up another friend on the way. Two other neighbor women drove their own cars or carpooled with other neighbors, since their workdays started somewhat later. Frances's aunt, uncle, and cousin drove forty miles up the mountain after work to see their new relative, bringing flowers and a gift wrapped in floral pink paper, and spent their visiting time deciding whose nose, mouth, and eyes Elizabeth had.

After visiting hours were over, Ruby stopped in on her way home to greet the new neighbor and to comfort the still-exhausted mother. Telling of her own childbearing experiences, Ruby related that her mother had said, "First you think you're going to die, then you're sure you're going to die, then just about the time you know you're dying, its all over." She offered both praise for the health of the child and comfort, suggesting that the second one always was easier; in fact, she almost didn't make it to the hospital with her second son, he had come so fast.

After two days in the hospital, Frances and baby returned home, where first one grandmother and then the other stayed to help with the baby and take care of the housework. Frances's sister, brother-in-law, niece, and nephew drove the three-hour trip to visit on the weekend, bearing gifts of clothes that were handed down from the nearly grown children. Her sister had bragged at work so much that coworkers said, "You'd think it was the sister who had had the baby." The two sisters giggled and talked for hours as Frances recounted each detail of the birth, and her sister held and rocked the baby. While they were there, an aunt, uncle, and cousin arrived, followed soon by Frances's father—her mother had been there all week. Despite the large gathering, Frances and Elizabeth were at ease. Surrounded by family intent on celebrating the new arrival, Frances felt safe and comfortable as the new baby was gently passed from one relative to the next. Even the cousins had their turn, and though closely supervised, held Elizabeth easily.

In the days that followed, mother, father, and baby began settling into a new routine at home and were visited by each close neighbor. Neighbor women and, occasionally, husbands as well, dropped in for a short visit, bringing delicate new baby things in pastel pink or white or yellow, telling their own special stories of the birth of their children. Sarah told of the tragic loss in childbirth of her first, beloved daughter and of their overwhelming joy in the birth of the twins.

Hazel told how each of her children came faster and faster. When her seventh arrived, she had jumped in the car and sped down the road, blowing the horn as she went roaring by her parents-in-law's store so they would be alerted and would track down her husband at work. She had parked in the middle of the emergency room lot and had yelled at the nurse on duty—"I'd be glad to fill out the forms, if you want me to have the baby right here in the hall!" The nurse relented, and just as she made it into the delivery room, John appeared.

Children are welcomed into home, family, and community as a gift from Heaven. News of their arrival travels quickly through the community, and their coming is celebrated by mother, father, siblings, cousins, aunts, uncles, grandparents, and nonkin neighbors alike. New fathers brag about the birth of the new daughter or son with reticent favor and awkward pride. Culturally, children are a source of joy, pride, and pleasure.

While the mother of a child conceived out of wedlock may suffer social stigma and bear tremendous guilt, the child is still viewed as a gift from Heaven and is welcomed, loved, and nurtured like any other child in the family and community. Abortion is unusual, and giving a child up for adoption is rare, occurring when the mother is isolated from kin. The sexual behavior of the parents has little bearing on the family's relationship to the child, although a young unwed mother frequently has difficulty establishing her role as mother of the child, since she is commonly in her mother's household and thus still considered a child herself. Mary Elizabeth said mockingly, "How often have I heard them say, 'She ain't got sense enough to look after that young 'un. I don't know what she'd have done if I wasn't here. She was foolish enough to go out and get herself pregnant . . . ' " Mary Elizabeth then added, "And I reckon I'd say the same thing myself if it was my young 'un."

The young child is the center of interest of the family, and discipline is minimal and sporadic. The mother is both the primary disciplinarian and the primary source of physical care, love, affection, and nurturance. The father is indulgent and affectionate yet distant, leaving most duties of physical care and discipline to the mother.

While the child's place in the center of the family is altered by the birth of a younger sibling or, at least beyond the nuclear family, diminishes somewhat in significance as he or she grows up, the love and affection of the family does not diminish. The family is a source of constant love and nurturance, and the child, growing to adulthood, rarely has cause either to alter the trust in the constancy of family or to question the reciprocation of that trust.

Young fathers and grandfathers alike take pleasure in piling the "least one" in the car beside them for a trip to a neighbor's or to the store as soon as the little one can walk. A ride on the tractor or lawnmower is a special treat for the toddler. Balanced precariously on his father's lap, the child is protected from a perilous fall by an encircling arm. Fathers and grandfathers gossip with their neighbors at the store about the toddler's latest exploits, and the old men frequently have a quarter ready to place in the child's palm if it can overcome its shyness long enough to approach the beckoning hand.

While fathers traditionally had little responsibility for care of young children, they enjoyed intimacy and play. Teasing was a special prerogative of older uncles and grandfathers in particular, who would nuzzle the children with scruffy whiskers until the little ones squealed with mixed fear and delight. When the teasing got too rough, these older men would embrace the little ones and comfort them, "pet" them, until their hearts were won back again.

While men were historically less involved with care of infants and young children, the increasing movement of women into the public work force, in combination with the increasing acceptance of male involvement with child care on the part of the media, is resulting in greater, though still limited, involvement of men with parenting. While women remain primary care givers, subtle changes are taking place.

Middle-aged women recall limited direct interaction with their fathers; fathers would take them to visit friends, to the store, to do business, or to show them off. More recently, thirty-four-year-old Junior Wilson cared for his preschooler, Billy, on a full-time basis because he was laid off and his wife was working full-time. As soon as Junior got a job, Billy started spending his days with his great-aunt, yet the year that they spent together created a special bond between Billy and Junior.

Fred Snyder's wife works full-time; since Fred got laid off, he spends most of the after-school time with one or more of his four children left in the home. He has always been quite close to his children and in his daily comings and goings in the community is rarely without a child or two. He has a particularly close relationship with his baby daughter. Now a lively nine-year-old, she suffered a serious illness as a preschooler, requiring frequent hospitalization and treatment by specialists. The whole family worked closely together to weather the crisis, and Fred spent a great deal of time worrying over and "petting" the baby. When his children were younger, Fred stood in the shadows just out of reach of the porch light on Halloween night as the children went trick-or-treating, or on occasion he knocked on the door himself as the small, costumed children clung to his trousers and the baby hid her painted face in his neck.

Fred is quite explicit about his life in the community. His family and his wife's family migrated north in the 1950s; though near neighbors at home, Fred and his wife met for the first time in Pennsylvania, married, and shortly after their second child was born, made the decision to come home. They knew the financial hardships they would face and the steady jobs they were leaving, but they wanted a way of life, a community, and in particular, an environment that they trusted in which to raise their children, one that seemed somehow better, healthier than what they had in Pennsylvania. And so they moved back and indeed struggled, with little education and with few jobs open to them. Their children thrived, as they did in their place in the community.

Virgil Stuart's store abounds with his offspring. His daughter and son and their spouses moved back home to try to make a life. All college graduates, several of Virgil's children moved away and stayed, yet these two decided to try it back home. The two women, the daughter and the daughter-in-law, help Virgil in the store; as the grandchildren have arrived, they have been nursed, rocked, and held in the store, have grown to the toddler age, and have learned all the secrets of the dustiest corners of the store. Virgil usually had a toddler in his arms, on his lap, or hiding behind his legs, and his affection for and ease with the children is readily apparent.

Sex-role differentiation begins at birth, as daughters in pink and sons in blue begin their indoctrination into American adulthood. Yet little differentiation was historically stressed until children were about five years of age or began to participate in minimal work activities. Children were definitely working members of their parents' households, and the young child was expected to perform tasks that contributed to household maintenance. As women's first realm of responsibility was and is the domestic sphere, young girls are taught to perform household duties, to help with meal preparation, housekeeping, and care of younger siblings. While young boys rarely do domestic chores, those whose families farm, dairy, keep livestock, or raise cash crops begin accompanying male family members about the property and are given small tasks for which they are responsible. With increasing age comes increasing responsibility and increasing reliance of the farming father on the young son.

Men have primary responsibility in most farm activities, whether full-time farming or part-time cash crops like tobacco, yet each family member plays an important role. Consequently, young girls and boys alike are valued workers, and girls grow up often participating in, sometimes responsible for, and generally minimally knowledgeable of, a variety of nondomestic tasks.

Traditionaly, a major sex-role difference in farm work was that women didn't run machinery, such as tractors, plows, balers, or mowing machines, as long as a male was available to do so.[1] Although young girls and boys both work at planting, hoeing, cultivating, and harvesting, only the boys are allowed to learn to drive the tractor. When J. B., his son Steve, his feeble older brother Henry, and his three grandchildren were harvesting hay together, the eight-year-old grandson got to drive the tractor, while his twelve-year-old sister was relegated to helping with the baling.

Although most farms are plowed by tractor, less common mule-drawn equipment is likewise the domain of men, as is the rare horse-drawn equipment. While historically men were responsible for plowing and harvesting with teams of horses or mules, women routinely knew how to handle the work and often worked the teams themselves. Twenty-eight-year-old Glenda Wilson says, "My mother never drove the tractor, but she did work with horses. Her daddy taught her, and Daddy taught me how to plow."

Turning of the land in the spring and plowing in preparation for planting is men's work. Planting of vegetable gardens is done by both men and women, although cash crops such as hay and corn are planted by men using mechanized equipment. Men and women working together transplant tobacco, although men generally operate any machinery used. Similarly, men tend the hay and corn cash crops when mechanized equipment is used, although women sometimes help load hay bales. Women and children may be hired to tend and harvest such cash crops as cabbages, beans, tomatoes, apples, and sometimes tobacco. Yet, especially with tobacco, harvesting and preparation for sale is done by men, women, and children, usually working together in extended-family groups. The care of vegetable gardens is primarily a task for women and children, as is the preparation of vegetables for winter storage.

In general, cash crops—with the exception of tobacco—are men's work, and home gardens are women's work. The planting and harvesting of cash crops are most often done with mechanized equipment; home gardens are tended without it. Tobacco is the one cash crop tended by men and women alike, although various aspects of planting, tending, harvesting, and marketing tobacco are sometimes divided according to sex. Thus where agriculture is mechanized, it is primarily men's work; where it is not, it is primarily women's work.

The rural woman thus grows up with little knowledge of machinery and is dependent on her male kin and neighbors to fix her car. As young boys are exposed early to the intricacies of a mechanical world, they routinely understand the workings of the family car, truck, lawn mower, tiller, or tractor while still in grammar school. Lucky is the boy whose responsibilities in a farm family include the privilege of driving the family's tractor on an important errand. Ralph Miller, reserved and bashful in his fifth-grade classroom, moves easily between his bicycle and the family tractor and handles the machinery with proud competence. Sallie Osborne, mother of three and school-bus driver, says she doesn't know much about cars beyond the battery and the spark-plug wires, but "it's a shame when a woman can't even change a flat tire, but there's a lot like that, you know."

Glenda Wilson says, "They'd let you throw hay bales and do the heaviest labor but not let you drive the tractor. I guess I got to drive it once, maybe twice. They wouldn't teach me how to drive the new tractor, but the old one that was all screwed up—the gears were a mess, and the brakes were all worn out." Women operated farm machinery only in extreme circumstances, "when there wasn't a man around to do it." Glenda continued, "Once I got to move the tractor twenty feet when there was no one else to do it. I only learned to go forward, though; never did learn reverse. The other time, it was going to rain, and Daddy, brother, and I were working together and we had to get the hay in. They had two tractors and put me on the smaller one because they had no other choice. I asked, but they never let me do it again."

Women did learn to operate machinery when it was necessary—"when there wasn't a man around to do it," and it was sometimes necessary. Daughters in a family with no sons, a young wife working with her young husband, a wife whose husband was away or ill, or a widow with no grown sons would step in to do what had to be done. Mary Elizabeth related, "I was sixteen when we got married and moved up on the mountain. We had eight head of cattle to feed, and although I hadn't driven a tractor before, we needed both of us driving the tractor that first winter. After that, I plowed and did whatever was necessary the whole time we were up there."

Historically women and girls were "protected" or restricted from exposure to animal breeding or birthing. Despite the varied activities on a farm related to animal husbandry, many older rural women have never witnessed an animal birth, even though they have lived their entire lives in a cattle-raising farm family. Glenda says, "We never were allowed to see breeding or birth or even slaughter of animals. Once when they were breeding a horse I wanted to go see the new horse they brought in for stud, but they wouldn't let me out of the house. But the eight-year-old boys were there. If there was a problem during a birthing and they needed help, they'd call a neighbor. I never knew anything about breeding or birthing. Mother would tell me a little about what was going on, but not much."

Mary Elizabeth added, "Of course we weren't supposed to go out there, but we'd see them breeding in the fields." In her family, "younger women didn't help with birthing animals, but older women would."

While women work in the slaughterhouses and a rare woman serves her neighborhood slaughtering and butchering animals on the farm, the processes relating to animal butchering are clearly segregated by sex. "The men would kill the cow, then we all went to work." Final preparation of the meat for storage was the realm of women.

Assigned chores are to be performed without delay. The need for each member of the family to contribute what he or she can to the family maintenance is so instilled in the young child that little fuss is normally raised over requests to perform expected household tasks or regular chores like milking, meal preparation, or feeding animals. In the middle of her conversation with a neighbor, Rebecca "hollered" to her twelve- and fourteen-year-old daughters to "get the hell out and get some wood" for the stove so that dinner might be prepared; they quickly ran out of the house and began splitting logs for kindling. About five minutes later they returned with a large load of wood, threw some of it into the stove, and took their places in the conversation. Their tasks completed, young boys and girls alike roam about the woods and creeks and the community in general, although girls stay closer to home.

Parental authority is firm and readily obeyed when it is expressed, but it is not frequently expressed. While some parents communicate requests to their children in a firm, calm manner, others routinely shout threats of violence. For these latter families, the bulk of the requests and threats are ignored, the child having a finely tuned sense of where the parent draws the line between "hollering" and final action. When the parent reaches the point of swatting at the child with a hand, the child may leap out of the way, laughingly avoiding the threat, while starting to take care of the requested chore.

Ralph Miller has assumed increasing responsibility in the family dairy since the fourth grade. With increasing responsibility have come increasing trust and freedom. A fifth grader, he drives the family tractor alone two miles down the road between home and the rented pasture where some of the cattle are grazed.

"Public work" brings financial remuneration and is a great boon to the family when it is available and when children can be freed for it. Agricultural activities do not restrict individuals, male or female, parents or children, from working jobs away from the home. Yet, incomes from these outside jobs are often indirectly contributed to the family. The nuclear family is the primary unit of production and consumption, and all other kin relations, as well as economic obligations, radiate outward from this primary unit into the rest of the community.

Ten-year-old Billy Wilson trudged up the road at the end of a hot summer afternoon and stopped to chat. "I'm plumb wore out," he boasted; "been working tobacco all day and made fifteen dollars." His pride in his newfound earning power was clear, and he looked forward to the next day's work. Thirteen-year-old Chris Weaver mows lawns for money around his obligations to help his father with the family's tobacco and garden. Since both parents work full time in public jobs, he must arrange the yard work around his father's work schedule and be available when he is home. Chris is saving his money for a ten-speed bicycle. Chris's father has given Chris and his two younger sisters a calf each to raise over the summer. Their father will charge them for the feed and any other expenses incurred, keeping a running tab over the summer. In the fall, he will buy each child's calf, paying according to the market price at the time, and then will collect each child's feed bill. Whatever remains is the child's earnings to do with as he or she sees fit. Their father will then take the fattened calves to market, and if the market price he gets differs from what he has paid his children, it is his gain or loss. Chris is keeping a close watch on the market.

Older children are not forced to assume cash-paying jobs outside the household but frequently desire them as an escape from the routine house- and farm-oriented tasks and as a means of obtaining extra luxury items and some degree of financial independence from the parents. Working children contribute goods and (rarely) cash to the nuclear family as long as they are living at home and may reserve some amount for their own use. They sometimes use their earnings to buy luxury items for the family, and especially for younger siblings. Those children who have cash-paying jobs are in turn relieved of many of their household duties.

Children quite frequently take jobs away from the home, often on neighbor's farms or businesses. When they are old enough, they tend to work in one of the factories located no less than fifteen miles away. A large portion of the income derived from these jobs will be contributed, directly or indirectly, to household maintenance. Children contribute cash to their parents on rare occasions; more commonly they contribute indirectly by purchasing food or clothing.

Fifteen-year-old Jimmy Blackwelder worked during the school year in his high school cafeteria; in addition to his small salary, he received free lunches. During the summer he tended a neighbor's tomatoes. In past years, Jimmy had worked both during the school year in after-school jobs and during the summer for several neighbors, performing tasks such as milking and feeding stock. His salary was his own, but he was responsible for most of his own clothing and for all of his entertainment. His two older brothers had finished high school and worked on a full-time basis, usually driving trucks for their father. They both had purchased cars and were completely responsible for all car expenses, including insurance, fines for violations, and maintenance and repair. Parents had no voice in decisions concerning the purchase of cars, except to express their dismay after the fact. The purchase and upkeep of cars demanded the largest outlays of money for these two young men. They were similarly responsible for their own clothng and entertainment, and from time to time they gave money to their mother for their food.

In another family, all of the older children had jobs as they were available. Timmy, Fred, and Jessie Mae had completed high school, and Timmy and Jessie Mae worked full time in a textile mill. Fred worked full time for his neighbor, a dairyman, who later provided a new trailer for Fred and his new wife, Pattie. The younger sister, Susie, who was still in high school, worked at various jobs, but because of her age and sex, she often was unable to find a job when she wanted one. She and her younger sister occasionally worked in tomatoes or tobacco for neighbors, but such work was seasonal and temporary. All of the children gave some of their earnings to their mother, and the older children bought whatever cars, clothing, luxury items, and entertainment they could afford. Timmy frequently purchased groceries for the family. On one occasion, after receiving an unexpected windfall from the sale of crops that he had planted and tended alongside the family's garden plot, he purchased several pieces of furniture for the house.

Parental authority becomes negligible for boys in their early teens; guidelines are still set, advice is given, threats of beatings and restrictions on activity are voiced, but rarely are they enforced. Relationships between father and son during this period are characterized by tension and restraint. Adolescent boys are expected to become functioning members of the male, extradomestic work unit, and if, in fact, boys participate willingly and energetically in men's activities, they reap the rewards of mature acceptance—they are treated as adults, included in camaraderie, joking, gossiping, and the world of male knowledge. Strain arises when sons are less enthusiastic participants in male work. Fathers who beat their sons run the risk of permanent enmity between themselves and their quasi-adult sons.

For girls, authority is minimally enforced during this period. In adolescence the relationship between father and daughter is characterized by distance due to the division of labor; working contact is minimal. By the time a daughter reaches her early teens, she is a competent, functioning member of the domestic work team. Particularly if she is an older sister of younger siblings, she is able to handle most of the daily affairs of the household, including, in particular, food preparation and care of younger siblings. By the middle-teen years, fathers have minimal control over their daughters. Fathers and daughters have little to do with each other. Fathers may occasionally issue laws and restrictions, but mothers intercede between fathers and daughters when necessary. In general, the teenage daughter is a quasi-adult member of the household. If the mother must be away from the household, she can leave the affairs of the house to the teenage daughter, particularly if the daughter is the oldest.

Mother-daughter relationships are relatively cooperative. Conflicts will be talked out, and more often than not, a teenage daughter will end up making her own decision about a particular course of action that her mother may not approve. Discussion will be long and earnest, but the daughter's decision is ultimately her own. This relationship of cooperation between mother and daughter steadily increases with age and maturity, although it commonly is fragmented dramatically—but only temporarily—by a daughter's marriage.

Mother-son relationships shift from parental authority and affection for young boys to a free-flowing, joking, and comradely relationship in adolescence. In fact, the influence of mothers over their sons, while shifting from maternal care to comradely advising, subtly increases with age. Particularly during late adolescence, while fathers have less control over their sons, a mother may carefully and gently intervene in crisis situations, not as an authority, but as a counselor or advisor.

As the communitywide public influence of men increases with age, an aged mother may be the only person who can actively, without hesitation or reservation, give advice or warning without risking confrontation. Sons often react playfully to an old mother's strong warnings or advice, but they rarely resent her interference with their business.

Clearly, children of a household are routinely contributing members of the nuclear-family economy. Furthermore, they are socialized quite early to expect and demand some degree of personal independence. As a result, they are prepared to make the logical step into marriage and toward independence from the parental household at early ages. With marriage comes independence within one's own new family unit.

MARRIAGE

Graduation at the high school was the ceremony signaling a new crop of adults into the world (or so the graduates thought), just as the first crops of early summer were beginning to mature. Girls wore pastel dresses with scrubbed and lightly made-up faces, stockings, and heeled sandals replacing the normal jeans and tennis shoes. Boys looked rather awkward in pressed shirts and ties, with clean-shaven faces and hair that could be of any length. An assortment of children—sisters, brothers, and cousins—moved wildly through the throng of gathered parents, grandparents, aunts and uncles, neighbors, and friends. Tears and sobs of friends, pierced by occasional yelps of joy or flirtation, contributed to the general hubbub.

Hazel and Bob, proud parents of the graduate—along with children George, Susan, Prissie, Ed, Fred, and John, and Bob's parents and assorted aunts, uncles, and friends—had come to watch Sarah and other graduating relatives march across the stage and into the world. Sarah had embraced each one of them, even her somewhat embarrassed but proud older brothers, and held John, "her baby," especially close; the tears streaked down her face when she hugged her mother and father. She made her exit quickly, stating that she wanted to go to the party at Patty's, where everyone would be, but she'd be sure to be in by midnight. She would go with her girlfriends who were waiting impatiently for her outside, she said. She had promised her mother not to go with her former boyfriend Dick, and Dick had not shown up for the ceremony.

Around midnight Hazel began to pace the living-room floor, debating in her anxious mind. She tried to convince herself that what she secretly feared would not happen. Sarah had gone to the party, she had had a good time visiting and laughing with her friends, they had lost track of the time in their exuberance, they had had a flat tire, they had run out of gas. As the minutes, then hours, ticked by, she became certain that her daughter was out of reach, no longer controllable, no longer the child. She was gone. She could not lock her up, threaten restrictions, or laugh with her as a daughter of the home. She was a wife, or soon to be, and there was nothing on earth that she could do to stop her. She was maybe already married to Dick.

Sarah had lied when she told them the week before that she had broken up with Dick, that she would go on to college. Hazel had wanted too hard to believe that Dick, Sarah's "fiancé," as Sarah liked to refer to him, was out of her life. He was weak, spoiled, a whiner, a city boy. His father was too rich; Dick was too crazy.

Around four o'clock Hazel approached the bedroom that Sarah and Prissie had shared for the eight years since they had built the new house. The one empty bed was a knife thrust into her gut. She flipped on the light, strode into the room, looked with horror into the now-empty closet, and shook the sleeping form of Prissie violently.

Like most of her older relatives, Sarah indeed had eloped. She had concealed her pregnancy from her close-knit family, with the exception of her younger sister, for four months. She chose elopement most likely because of her family's strong dislike of her fiancé, their high expectations for her higher education, and her strong desire to prove to them that she could have her marriage and her baby without their help. The oldest daughter in the large family, Sarah had long been able to run the household. She had taken over much of the baby's care, even moving him into her room when she was only nine herself. She knew how to garden, put up food, take care of her horses, prepare meals, shop for groceries, and clean the house and could manage not only her younger siblings but her older brothers as well. When she said "jump," they jumped, and she could arm wrestle her older brothers to a close draw if not a win. She knew how to earn money as well. She babysat, took care of several yards in the community, and worked the three summers when she was in high school in a local restaurant. She had successfully fought for her position there when she saw the management move a young man, new to the job, into the higher-paid position she wanted, in which she had substituted often enough to perform competently.

Unlike other relatives who had eloped, Sarah did not return home the next day or week. She waited until the baby was five months old, until she had firmly established her own family, before she came back home to show off the baby to the large group of welcoming kin.

Dick was certainly no stranger in Sarah's household. He had been part of the family for two years, a participant in birthdays, Christmas activities, meals, and family celebrations of all sorts; he had helped garden, put up hay, and mow the yard; he participated in family fights and had played with the younger brothers and sisters, taking them skating, to movies, and out for treats at the store.

While formal dating is not uncommon in the rural community, particularly as consolidated high schools have brought urban dating patterns to the rural areas, courting for most rural young people is still a family affair, taking place within sight of family members. Boys come to visit and "hang out" with the girl and her family, or they visit with their current or would-be girlfriends at school or on their way home from school on the bus.

Events to which couples might go on a date, either alone or with another couple, include movies, bowling, or roller skating, or they may just "ride around," meeting other carloads of young people who are doing the same thing. Rural high school students attend high school ball games, yet only a few attend school dances.

Though elopement was quite common until recent years, church weddings have become the norm in a mere decade. School consolidation, mass communication, an influx of immigrants, and in general, changing values have contributed to an almost total turnabout in the past decade with respect to marriage. Mary Jane notes, "It's the girls that want the weddings; they get the idea from their friends at school. Even the poor girls want a church wedding." Whereas twenty and even ten years ago a young couple would secretly elope, or even take a parent with them to sign for a minor daughter, the new pattern is the church wedding, "the dress, the flowers, the whole bit," with all the family members in attendance.

The newlywed couple is expected to establish a new household. Because elopement allowed little planning and because of the scarcity of housing, a newly married couple usually resided temporarily with the parents of either spouse until other living arrangements could be made. Historically, young married couples resided close to one spouse's parents, often in a house built on the parent's land. Because of the high cost of building, this alternative is increasingly unavailable, although mobile homes, which can be obtained with minimal down payments, allow many young couples to continue this traditional and convenient residence pattern.[2]

J. O. and Jane moved into their new, factory-furnished mobile home shortly after they were married. J. O. relates, "Well, we wanted to stay pretty close around here, 'cause after I get off work at the water department in town, I help Daddy farm, and we know folks around here." Jane added, "J. O.'s mom wanted us to put the trailer almost in their yard, but we told her we'd rather be up here on the hill." "Up here on the hill" is a beautiful spot on a gravel road on the eighty-six-acre farm that J. O. and his father work. J.O.'s parents live about a quarter mile away, across the hill. J.O. continued, "Daddy let us pick out the place we wanted to set up on. He would have let us build a house if we'd wanted to, but after we looked at the cost of building a house, plus buying furniture, we just figured we could get by better with a trailer."

For young couples like J.O. and Jane, with a combined family income of less than fifteen thousand dollars, mobile-home residence close to family members helps stretch the family budget. Cooperative labor, readily available child care, shared resources, full access to an unlimited supply of wood fuel, garden space, and rent-free land greatly enhanced their twenty-thousand-dollar mobile-home investment.

HUSBANDS AND WIVES

A man is a full participant in the community, a social adult, through his role as husband and father, and a woman comes into her own as a wife and mother. People rarely remain unmarried, yet to do so is regretfully accepted for those who have stayed home to care for aging parents.

Open displays of affection between husbands and wives are never seen in public and only on rare occasions seen by children within the home. While the weekly letters of the young soldier to his bride during World War II express a depth of affection, love, and devotion, this affection will never be seen or expressed in public.

The complementary roles of husbands and wives confine each to a distinct realm of activity. The husband is the public spokesman for the family among other men. Yet he is dependent on his wife for daily needs, comfort, and the warmth that their home represents. Within their home, the husband seldom interferes with the activities of the wife, and her independence gives her considerable informal power within this realm.

The public and private roles of husband and wife differ dramatically. The wife rarely interrupts or contradicts her husband in public and defers to his position as authority and spokesman. In public places, husbands and wives often sort themselves out, husbands conversing with other men and wives seeking the company of women. Yet in private, their relationship is relaxed, and the joking, warmth, or even hostility of husband and wife is more readily expressed. A woman may disagree with her husband in private and may argue forcefully and convincingly for a point about which she would not contradict him in public.

With a deep sense of the complementary nature of their roles and of the obligations of a good man toward his family and their needs, the wife accepts the authority of her husband as a natural fact of life. She relies on him for financial support for herself and her children, for consideration of her emotional and physical needs, for negotiating the public world of community on behalf of the family, and for defending and protecting the family against harm. She respects his will and his authority, never disputing him in public. Her own ability to manipulate or circumvent that will and to retain her independence within her own realm of responsibility, her ever-increasing power as she moves through the life cycle, and the prospering of her family are her compensation.

The warmth and affection of husband and wife can be expressed more comfortably by the elderly. The rich repertoire of their shared work and experiences, their different views and recollections of events that they observed together, the shared joys in a daughter's marriage and children, the tragedy of a son's untimely death, or the intrigues of a complicated family matter provide much material to share with each other and with others. As he grows older, the husband's participation in the public affairs of the community, and thus his authority, diminish, and he spends less time in productive labor and more time close to home. The wife's position in the home and family increases in importance as she ages, and the "old woman" is clearly on an equal footing with her "old man." They spend more time together and more time together with others, visiting relatives and neighbors.

Maxine and Cecil, now in their seventies and retired from their storekeeping days, put out a garden together and keep a few head of cattle, but their days of farming ninety acres, raising chickens, storekeeping, and being involved in politics are over. They go to town together at least once a week to shop for groceries or for a doctor's appointment and to visit old friends and share the latest gossip. When a neighbor started a pick-your-own strawberry patch, Cecil drove them out early in the morning to pick several gallons, an activity in which he wouldn't have engaged in his younger years. He even helped cap the strawberries and kept the fire stoked in the old wood stove they used for canning and, in the winter, for making freezer jam. She doesn't can so much any more, but they still like to have enough on hand for the frequent visits from their children and grandchildren.

Maxine and Cecil spend most of their time together now around home. They go to church regularly, always vote on election day, and enjoy stopping in at the store to discuss politics. They like to collect ginseng and dig the rare roots in the special places only they know about. When neighbors stop in to visit, a cup of coffee and a piece of cake are always available; if Maxine is not prompt enough in offering refreshments, Cecil jokingly scolds her not to let the visitors starve. They spend most evenings watching television, and the lore from the media combines with current community events and history to produce a diverse repertoire of stories. Yet their storytelling styles differ, and they frequently interrupt each other to correct a date or to add a significant detail. The interruptions themselves become a focus in the exchange as they banter back and forth about who's telling the story and who's growing forgetful.

SEX ROLES AND RESIDENCE PATTERNS

The marriage of children and the death of parents are the primary ways in which the nuclear family unit is changed and new units formed. When all the children have left the parents' household, the parents continue to reside alone if they are able, although in close proximity to other kin. Because close kin are residentially clustered, relatives are usually nearby to meet the needs of an old couple. Even in extreme old age or infirmity, where daily attention is required, a married couple will continue to reside alone if at all possible.

Older widows, whose children have all left home, frequently live alone, yet in close proximity to helping kin. Mary Snyder, now in her eighties, lives in her trailer where the old house stood. Her two daughters grew so alarmed that their nearly blind mother would fall trying to negotiate the narrow steps that they had the house torn down and replaced by the trailer. Mary lives alone now, yet next door to her daughter and son-in-law, who look in on her daily. Her daughter works full time in a mill twenty miles from the house and is gone during the day, yet her son-in-law, now retired from his job as a school janitor down the mountain, which kept him away from early Monday morning until late Friday night, is a frequent visitor. Sometimes Mary fixes lunch for him and for a neighbor who is helping him mend fences and the like, and sometimes he brings lunch over to Mary's. While her mobility is limited by her failing eyesight, she keeps in contact with the goings-on in the community by telephone, visiting daily with her one surviving sister, her daughter, and other women friends in the community. Across the road lives her son-in-law's mother, Lucy, now in her late nineties. Kinship, friendship, neighborliness, and probably an element of competition bound them closely through the years, yet they communicate rarely and indirectly now. Lucy has grown increasingly deaf, but they could still visit, for Mary could hear Lucy and then write out responses and questions. Lucy is visited daily by her son across the road, her daughter who lives in one trailer, or by another son who lives in another trailer next door.

While women often live alone, men rarely do. Besides the greater longevity of women, this pattern results from the sexual division of labor and the differing socialization of men and women. J.B. Blackwelder, who was unusually considerate of his wife, beamed with pride the morning he made coffee for the first time in his life. His wife was ill, and he insisted that she should not get up to fix his breakfast as usual. At the age of sixty, J.B. had never cooked anything, and the success of the coffee was an important achievement. There is general agreement that a man alone cannot, and should not be expected to, take care of his own domestic needs. Even when a woman leaves the community for overnight visits elsewhere, her husband will sometimes go to his mother's or to another relative's house to stay for the duration of the wife's absence, or his mother or another female relative may come in to cook and clean for him, if there are no daughters old enough to assume these responsibilities.

The five men who stopped in at the store on their way to work picked up an assortment of supplies—cups of coffee, a cake, a honey bun, a pouch of chewing tobacco—and then stood waiting around the doorway as young Will wandered about the store. He finally completed his shopping and laid his selection on the counter to be rung up: an oatmeal cookie, a sandwich, two bags of chips, a candy bar, a pint of milk, a can of vienna sausages, a pack of crackers, and a bottle of Pepto-Bismol. As the others waited, they looked at the pile on the counter and one said, "You going to work or you going to sit and eat all day?" Another added, "We ain't gonna get no work out of him today." Will said, "Yeah, boys, I'm just going to sit under a big tree and watch you'uns work." Then he added quietly, "My old lady will be coming home from her mother's tomorrow."

A child who does not marry, yet remains in the community, normally stays with his or her parents, regardless of age. Forty-six-year-old Richard has always lived with his parents and continues to live with his widowed mother. Neighbors expect that Richard will, or at least should, marry after his mother dies. The man who lives alone is considered an oddity, as was suggested by accounts of the very few men in the three communities who had died alone. All help is given to the very few young bachelors in the community who, past the age of about thirty, are pitied for their inability to find a wife, and/or are suspected of various sorts of potential mental instability for not wanting one. The old man who lives alone may in fact demonstrate to the community his mental instability through his pitiable condition, as his dwelling is often rude, simple, and perennially cold, his clothing is filthy, and his health is sometimes bad from poor dietary habits.

If a wife dies leaving young children, the husband may have an unmarried daughter, sister, or other female relative live with him. This arrangement occurs if no daughters in the home are old enough to care for the house or if all the daughters have left the house. In such a case the relative who moves in may stay with the widower until he dies or remarries.

Indeed, widower remarriage seems relatively common. Two cases were recorded in one community in which a young wife died leaving one child; in one case the husband's brother's family raised the son and in the other case the wife's parents raised the son. In two other similar situations a female relative of the husband lived with the family until he remarried. One unmarried widower was Charles Phillips, whose children were all married or working elsewhere and had left the household. Upon his wife's death, their unmarried daughter returned to the community to live with her father and to take care of him in his old age. She was expected to stay with him until his death.

Divorced women with children may stay with their parents for a time or may continue to live separately. Women generally live alone in widowhood, and the unmarried woman who stays at home to look after her parents until they die is not uncommon. The daughter usually inherits the parents' house and a significant portion of the land. Her position as head of her household and as resident and owner of "the homeplace" places her in an important social position in her family and in the community. She often does the work of men, that is, "public work" in order to support herself; she may hire people with whom she works her land and may supervise her male relatives who come to assist her. She may take an active role in local politics and speak her mind in social gatherings like those that occur spontaneously yet regularly in the local store.

AGE AND CHANGING POWER

For both husband and wife, middle age is a time of hard work, of greatest productivity, of greatest financial need, and of greatest economic activity. Men reach the height of their public influence in late middle age. They have the stamina and strength—albeit waning—for all important activities of youth, but tempered by good sense and self-control. Opinions are offered with confidence; they have the repertoire of the past; that is, they know about people and events and have done things about which the young know little. Yet they can still do the work of younger men. They have the advantage of seeing both generations around them—the old and the young—in a culturally defined, "sensible" perspective. They have the wisdom and expertise from the past, which can influence and temper new input from the present; cultural definitions of rationality and reason are epitomized by this period of life; impetuousness is waning. Stamina, expertise, and patience combine to lend to the middle-aged man an air of importance. Opinions offered are most readily acknowledged, credibility is at its highest, emotional and psychological maturity are finally achieved and—more important—publicly acknowledged. Self-confidence is at its highest and is reinforced by public recognition.

Women during this period are sometimes depressed. Hard work of an earlier age and of the present begets more work and the most difficult period of adjustment—the loss of children from the home. Domination by the husband is at its peak, while the psychological rewards of submission are at their lowest. The romance of youth is gone and the drudgery of middle age is overwhelming. Although children may be establishing their homes and families nearby, they are simultaneously and emphatically cutting their ties of dependence with home and mother, and the ties of "mature dependence" and cooperation will not be established until they begin having children and settling into their own nuclear-family formation and economic consolidation. This time is one of greatest distress for women, and it appears to be culturally induced by patterns of family development and the sexual division of labor.

For men, old age is the period of declining influence. Physical stamina is waning, and opinions, technical expertise, and those factors that combine to create public credibility are becoming dated. In limited spheres of activity and expertise, old age does guarantee influence, but in general, public influence diminishes markedly. Old men are publicly respected but patronized. Old age is culturally respected by canons of polite behavior, but relationships are generally dominated by patronizing old men for their knowledge and expertise in limited areas. The work of men is passing them by, and they have been replaced by the next generation, who have gradually but competently assumed the power.

For women, old age is the time of consolidation of power. Women's work, which is crucial for basic daily survival and comfort, never ceases even in old age, although because of the easing of responsibilities due to departure of children from the home, work may become more creative. Long-abandoned handwork and the like may be resumed. Public influence may in fact be achieved through the ever-strengthening relationship with grown sons, who may be approaching or enjoying their prime, or directly through widowhood.

In the domestic sphere, influence through expertise and experience is finally acknowledged, as grown daughters have their own families and are aware of the extent of their need for help and of the limitations of their own experience. "Mature dependence" on the part of children is achieved, and finally, old women are privately and publicly acknowledged for their expertise. Recognition of expertise breeds self-confidence, and mountain women gain self-confidence through aging.

Adjustment to the death of a spouse is quite divergent because of sex-role differences in status and personal expertise. While the widower is particularly pitiable because of his forced reliance on women for basic daily needs, the widow may become the epitome of self-confidence and wit, one who is above the strivings of youth, relatively independent, and in total control for the first time in her life. To some extent, the older widow may in fact defy the norms of polite deference in proffering opinions, or even the norms of decency, since she is above criticism. The old "widder woman" is a predominant figure in mountain humor, and for good reason. She can, and may, enjoy the sexual innuendo, with of course younger men and women being the butt of her remarks. Several observers have noted the personality alteration that a widow seems to undergo after an appropriate period of mourning—the quiet, unassuming, unopinionated, deferential lady becomes aggressively opinionated and, perhaps, even raucous. She is above rebuke, and the badge of old age is worn with pride and confidence.

Evidence of the apparent power shift between the sexes in

old age is found in mountain folklore, where the "widder woman" is a relatively common and ambiguous character, a trickster. The "old crone" is rarely generous, although she appears alternatively as the seer, the herb doctor, or the witch. She possesses wisdom, evil, power, or truth—but rarely goodness; the sweet old grandma is symbolically irrelevant. Conversely, old men are rarely portrayed in any fashion, occurring occasionally as god figures, such as the wise old men in the Jack Tales. Dirty old men and male tricksters do not occur in mountain folk literature. No ambiguity is associated with aging masculinity, nor is any humor.

Religious participation and expression likewise reflect shifting power relationships between the sexes. In rural Appalachian communities, as in any society, religious institutions serve a variety of functions, an important one being the sublimation and relief of anxiety. Accordingly, women's participation in religious activity reaches greatest intensity in middle age, during the time when social events are least satisfying and stress is greatest. Furthermore, religious participation by women does not generally increase with aging. Conversely, for men the primary function of the church during middle age is the public arena it provides; the church is to some degree an extension of the political sphere of activities and a forum for determining public consensus. For men in old age, however, conversion or religious intensification may be significant. As public influence wanes, religious expression quite often increases. Several old men who were notorious in their younger days for excessive drinking, sexual prowess, fearlessness, violence, and general "meanness" had become extremely devout and pious, interspersing scripture and conversion messages with their church-oriented description of the events of the world.

HISTORICAL RETROSPECTIVE

For about a century, writers have presented conflicting images of the social roles and relationships of mountain women and men. While journalists and local-color writers around the turn of the century describe Appalachian society as patriarchal, a multitude of relationships are subsumed under this term. Julian Ralph, writing in 1903, describes mountain women as drudges, slaving their youth away, while men enjoy the fruits of their labor:

> The girls are often married at thirteen. Marriages at fourteen or fifteen are very common, and a girl of twenty is considered an old maid and ineligible if she has younger sisters. What I have seen of the girls and whatever I have heard of them and their mothers has roused my pity. The oldest daughter in one of these always large mountain families is almost certain to begin her life of drudging while very young, and as the women are all drudges after marriage and are married in childhood, drudging is their lot until they die.
>
> They do all the work of cabin and farm, excepting during the few days at harvest-time, when the men help to garner the crops. They bear very many children: they cook, wash, mend, weave, knit, plough, hoe, weed, milk the cows, and do practically all else that is to be done. The men loaf about on horseback along the roads, visit their neighbors, the store, and the nearest village, and have as good and easy a time as they know how. [P. 41]

Horace Kephart's descriptions, based on more detailed observations over extended periods of time, still reiterate this dichotomy of the mountain patriarch and the wife as drudge. In 1913 he wrote "It is a patriarchal existence. The man of the house is lord. He takes no orders from anybody at home or abroad. Whether he shall work or visit or roam the woods with dog and gun is nobody's affair but his own. About family matters he consults with his wife, but in the end his word is law" (1976:530).

However, Kephart's description, as well as his references to specific instances of husband-wife interaction, suggests a little more depth: " 'The woman,' as every wife is called, has her kingdom within the house, and her man seldom meddles with its administration. Now and then he may grumble 'A woman's allers findin' somethin' to do that a man can't see no sense in'; but then, the Lord made women fussy over trifles—His ways are inscrutable—so why bother about it?" (1976:331). Finally, Kephart reveals something more about the value system from which he writes as he notes "woman's weakness" and laments the lack of chivalry in the treatment of women by men:

> Outside the towns no hat is lifted to maid or wife. A swain would consider it belittled his dignity. At tables, if women be seated at all, the dishes are passed first to the men; but generally the wife stands by and serves. There is no conscious discourtesy in such customs; but they betoken an indifference to woman's weakness, a disregard for her finer nature, a denial of her proper rank, that are real and deep-seated in the mountaineer. To him she is little more than a sort of superior domestic animal. The chivalric regard for women that characterized our pioneers of the Far West is altogether lacking in the habits of the backwoodsman of Appalachia. [1976: 331-32]

John C. Campbell, whose *Southern Highlander and His Homeland* was first published in 1921, avoids using the term "patriarchal," describing instead the sexual division of labor and the different socialization of boys and girls. Campbell makes a distinction, suggested above by Kephart, between the realms of authority of men and women:

> Down (the road) the man of the household finds his way to store or mill, to the neighboring hamlet and the county-seat; but the woman, especially if she lives up a smaller branch or away at the head of the hollow, is very much shut in. Home duties and the care of the children tie her closely, and the difficulties of travel during long seasons of the year serve still further to limit her to her immediate neighborhood. She has little to do with politics, and little to do with the management of church affairs save when occasion calls to prepare a bounteous repast for the visiting preacher and the many friends

who come to hear him. Her place is the home, and in the home the relations of man and woman are Pauline. [1969:124]

While contrasting the "favored [status] . . . dignity, [and] conscious superiority" (1969:124) of boys with the "painful path of mountain womanhood" (1969:126) that girls must tread, Campbell describes the status of older mountain women in lofty terms:

> There is something magnificent in many of the older women with their stern theology—part mysticism, part fatalism—and their deep understanding of life. Patience, endurance, and resignation are written in the close-set mouth and in the wrinkles about the eyes; but the eyes themselves are kindly, full of interest, not unrelieved by a twinkling appreciation of pleasant things. "Granny"—and one may be a grandmother young in the mountains—if she has survived the labor and tribulation of her younger days, has gained a freedom and a place of irresponsible authority in the home hardly rivaled by the men of the family. Her grown sons pay to her an attention which they do not always accord their wives; and her husband, while he remains still undisputed master of the home, defers to her opinion to a degree unknown in her younger days. Her daughters and her grandchildren she frankly rules. Though superstitious she has a fund of common sense, and she is a shrewd judge of character. In sickness she is the first to be consulted, for she is generally something of an herb doctor, and her advice is sought by the young people of half the countryside in all things from a love affair to putting a new web in the loom.
>
> It is not surprising if she is something of a pessimist on the subject of marriage. "Don't you *never* get married," is advice that is more likely to pass her lips . . . .
>
> Now at last she has leisure to enjoy herself as never before. If vigorous she likes to fish on the bank of the neighboring creek, and she is no mean fisherman, as her

catch will prove. She is partial to company and to strange tales of new lands and new places—wants to see them too. One meets her sometimes going a-visiting, not mounted in the shameful new fashion which is creeping in even among her children, but sedately side-saddle, her full skirt and striped apron ruffled about her feet, a red kerchief around her neck, her hands encased in woolen mits. She has perhaps a clay pipe tucked deep down in her pocket, with a twist of home-cured tobacco raised on her own hillside. Under the big sunbonnet or gay handkerchief or "fascinator" her brown and weather-beaten face peers sharply but serenely out on a world which she has no longer reason to fear.

Old age has indeed its compensations both for men and women, more worth-while here in the mountains, perhaps, than in many places more urban and sophisticated. It has at least the respect of the younger generation and the dignity of labor achieved. [1969: 140-41]

Emma Bell Miles, writing in 1905, describes the nature of her relatives' lives in the mountain communities surrounding Chattanooga, Tennessee. Miles, like Campbell, suggests a distinctly different pattern of behavior that men and women exhibit as they move through the life cycle: "The best society in the mountains—that is to say, the most interesting—is that of the young married men and that of the older women" (1975:36). Elaborating on the mountain woman, she continues:

It is not until she has seen her own boys grown to be men that she loses entirely the bashfulness of her girlhood, and the innate beauty and dignity of her nature shines forth in helpfulness and counsel.

I have learned to enjoy the company of these old prophetesses almost more than any other. The range of their experience is wonderful; they are moreover, repositories of tribal lore—tradition and song, medical and religious learnings. They are the nurses, the teachers of practical arts, the priestesses, and their wisdom commands the respect of all. [1975:37]

On the power relationship, Miles notes: "An old woman has usually more authority over the bad boys of a household than all the strength of man. A similar reverence may have been accorded to the mothers of ancient Israel, as it is given by all peoples to those of superior holiness—to priests, teachers, nuns; it is not the result of affection, still less of fear" (1975:37-38).

The writings of Kephart, Campbell, and Miles thus all suggest a significant pattern in the distribution and meaning of influence and power as men and women move through the life cycle.

SEX ROLES AND INDUSTRIALIZATION

Women's primary realm of responsibility can be viewed as the domestic or familial realm, while that of men, the extra-domestic or public.[3] For the rural family in western North Carolina, the domestic sphere traditionally included primary responsibility for children and home, clothing, food purchases, storage and preparation of food, gardening, and a variety of related activities mentioned throughout this description. The male, extradomestic realm included cash crops, public work, and associations with other men that may be considered the public affairs of the community. The female, domestic realm was culturally construed as subordinate to the authority of the male, public realm.

Within this system of culturally defined, sex-role inequality, women have more or less formal authority, depending on their point in the life cycle, the composition of the residential unit they may or may not share with others, their economic situation, and their individual personalities and abilities to manipulate others in positions of power or authority.

Prior to the turn of the century, the coming of the railroads, and the beginnings of industrialization in the mountains, Appalachian communities consisted primarily of yeoman farm families. An egalitarian social order and fairly rigid sexual division of labor appear to have been characteristic.

Industrial development in the mountains began to alter the nature of the society, most dramatically during the period from 1880 to 1930. Timbering, mining, and trading took men away from the farm for a few days, weeks, months, or even years at a time. While the migration of rural families from Appalachia accelerated after World War II, men alone and men with their families were traveling or moving out to become temporary or full-time wage earners in the early 1900s.

While little concrete information is available on the sexual division of labor prior to the industrialization process, writers since the turn of the century suggest a flexible division of labor within a broadly defined distinction between male and female domains. Industrialization of the labor force, though unevenly felt throughout the area, seems to have contributed to greater flexibility in sex-role definition.[4] As men increasingly entered the public labor market, their families absorbed their work on the family farm. Their wives and children took responsibility for running the mill, plowing the fields, harvesting and marketing produce, clearing new ground, butchering livestock, felling trees and mending fences.

For men, the vicissitudes of the family economy have demanded flexibility and participation in the public labor force. Work histories of older men are characteristically varied. Older men commonly worked in timber and perhaps in mining; many journeyed out to find work in northeastern industry, in western timber, and in a range of other occupations. Women were expected to take up the slack as men moved in and out of the public labor market.

The family's shifting economic viability in an industrializing larger society, the decreasing profitability of agriculture in the mountains, and the increasing cost, value, and tax base of rural land have all contributed to the decline of the family farm; these factors have thus worked to decrease the rural family's control over production and to increase the family's reliance on the public labor market. As men became wage earners, women's roles within the subsistence farming family became more flexible.

In the 1950s, small textile mills began to be a major employer of women, increasing in importance through the 1970s. The movement of women into the labor force in large numbers, increasing since the 1950s, has affected family life, sex roles, women's status, the socialization of children, and family farming activities. Small textile mills, a major employer for women in the mountains, hire women from farm families whose farm incomes need buttressing. The income of women is usually critical to the family, especially for the farming family or for those families in which the husband is laid off. The number of women in professions—nursing, teaching, social services, mental health—or in secretarial positions is small, while the majority of working women are blue-collar factory workers. The textile mills in particular hire women because women "are willing or perhaps unable to be unwilling to take secondary jobs."[5] For rural mountain women, particularly unskilled workers, the job alternatives are few to nonexistent, increasingly so in the early 1980s. The textile industries are characterized by low wages, poor working conditions, arbitrary discipline, and no career ladders, and the local male labor force is simply denied access to the production-line jobs.

Women in rural communities, while limited by the types of employment available to them, in addition face the burden of the "double day." After a full shift in public work, they face full responsibility for all of the traditionally female work of home and farm. Women are ultimately responsible for home and children whether they have outside paid employment or not.

With public work, the role of women in the family and community is being altered, and new patterns are being tested. Women gain power in the allocation of household resources and increase their influence over the decisions in the community, particularly in education and health care. Their constant association with other working women with different social backgrounds, goals, and expectations provides exposure to new ideas and a setting for airing grievances and for exploring new ideas about women's work, roles, and responsibilities. For some, divorce has been the consequence. For others, the result has been a less well kept house, more fast foods, and more store-bought clothes. For still others, a greater sharing of domestic responsibilities with husband has been a result. Yet for most, myriad frustrations have yet to be resolved.

The burden on the husband of the working wife is quite real, since his ability to support his family is called into question. Ed Miller, his wife, Evelyn, and their two sons had to make a critical family decision: either Ed could take a job and they would give up the family dairy or Evelyn would go to work and Ed and the boys could maintain the dairy. They agreed together that Evelyn would go to work, and she did so willingly; now the boys spend much of their spare time before and after school, on weekends, and during the summer working the dairy.

When Junior Wilson was laid off, he took full responsibility for his preschool son, Billy, since his wife was working full-time. While Junior's lunch fare was simple, his relationship to Billy was close and nurturant, and Billy followed Junior on his frequent jaunts around the neighborhood. However, Junior explained his role as primary care giver with reluctance and guilt.

A final dimension to the issue of women and public work involves the implications of the type of employment available to women. As women move into the labor market, they are assuming a variety of low-status, low-wage jobs and may in fact be suffering a loss of status in the public sector as compared with their traditional economic and social roles in the rural community. Thus while the ability to earn a living brings with it some measure of personal freedom, the kind of work that women must do is drudgery, demoralizing, boring, and stressful (particularly if they must meet production quotas); it truly makes women second-class citizens in the wider industrial society. The trend in Appalachia is consistent with a broad trend in many industrializing regions of the world, namely, the use of women as a source of cheap labor and the resulting deterioration in their situation.[6]

The rural agricultural heritage, subsistence orientation, cooperative sharing by the extended family in production, complementary roles in marriage, fluid sex roles, and the historical legacy of a relatively egalitarian social order required the full, though flexible, participation of women in productive labor. Despite economic exploitation of women in the public labor market, working-class consciousness is only slowly emerging, particularly among women. A strong sense of rootedness in place, identification with and reliance on extended-family ties, as well as a sense of history in the community combine with a sense of purpose and role in the family and community. From that experience have come confidence, a strong sense of personal identity, and recognition of the importance of women's contribution to home, family, and community.

Chapter Five

FOREIGNERS

LINDA AND LARRY DOUTHIT, "hippies" at first, who would later grow into neighbors, moved into Rocky Creek in 1971. They found their forty-two acres and house through the *Agricultural Review.* They bought their place for seven thousand dollars when the good deals on land could still be made and, despite irregular and minimal incomes, managed to have it paid for by 1975.

The Douthits had purchased their place from the estate of Maggie Wiseman through a lawyer in Brownsville and therefore had had only brief contact with their closest neighbors, the Blackwelders. They began the arduous task of clearing out piles of debris, left from years of careless renters. Accumulated garbage was piled high inside and outside the house, and two abandoned cars were in the yard.

Several weeks passed with no contact with neighbors. Their house was out of sight of the road, and the Douthits paid little attention to the neighbors as they stayed busy coming and going—to town for cleaning and household supplies, to the local store for ice cream or a soda, or to the dumpster with yet another load of trash.

Linda and Larry later discovered that their neighbors had been quite aware of their presence, their activities, and their attempts to make the ramshackle house livable and attractive. Maggie Wiseman, who had built the house and lived in it until her death, had been close kin and friend to many of the neighbors. Her beautiful flowers had graced the then-neat, sturdy, frame-and-plaster house. Linda and Larry not only cleared the inside of the house of debris, washing walls and floors as they proceeded, but began rescuing the yard and flowers from the weeds, winning the silent approval of the neighborhood.

On the third Saturday morning after the Douthits started their serious work on the house, J.B. Blackwelder and his son Mark appeared in the driveway, J.B. driving a half-ton truck, and Mark a front-end loader. They offered help in clearing away the cars and other debris, which the Douthits gratefully accepted, and J.B. and Mark hauled them away.

Because Linda and Larry moved in the spring, they began to "make a garden." The garden spot had not been worked for several years, and they had only a pushplow and hoes with which to turn the soil. The work was difficult, but one afternoon when they came home from shopping in town they found their garden spot had been plowed—by their neighbor J.B.

Andy and Frances moved into their house during the lull between early January snowstorms. They moved in on a Tuesday, and on the next Saturday a new, eight-inch snowfall blanketed the community. They were awakened that morning by the sound of a bulldozer and ran to the window to see a neighbor whom they had not met plowing out their driveway.

Newcomers to the community are welcomed by cautious gestures of neighborliness. While none comes to call at first, neighbors will stop to chat if they are passing by and see some activity in the yard or will wave as they drive by. A slow, steady process of incorporating newcomers will gradually emerge, as bits of information are exchanged and offers of assistance begin to be given.

On the community side, each bit of information about the newcomers is passed among neighbors, and a composite picture slowly emerges—where the newcomers are from, how many (if any) children they have, where they work and what they do there, whether they've bought the house or are renting, how old they are, whether they're summer people, renters, retirees, permanent, or seasonal, what kind of car they drive, and generally, how they're going to fit in. Later, the newcomers will be invited to attend the local churches.

Andy and Frances had several long conversations with the

neighbor from whom they bought their land. They stopped in for purchases at the local store, and they chatted with the mailman. Andy talked with a neighbor who stopped his car when he saw Andy in the yard, mostly discussing the weather. Yet Frances was surprised, several weeks after they moved in, to realize that a stranger who stopped in front of the house as she was walking to her car knew her name and occupation and how long they had been in the house.

As gestures of neighborliness are offered, they will increase in magnitude if they are appropriately received. If the gestures are well received, if the newcomer takes the time to talk, trade stories, and show interest, then conversations will increase with more and more neighbors. Neighbor women, after a time, will drop by to offer a gift of pickles just canned, a couple of ripe tomatoes just off the vine, a quart of honey just collected, or apples just picked. If the neighbors are invited in, they'll stay and chat for a while and leave with the standard departure, "Let's go up to the house," or, "Come and see us." As neighbors learn of the newcomers' needs, these will be relayed around the community. Likewise, pieces of the community, brief anecdotes about people in the community, and the past history of their land or house will be shared.

In the past, few newcomers came to the rural mountain communities. The 1960s, however, saw the increasing popularity of the mountains for second-home development. In increasing numbers, "summer people," or "Florida people," began to locate land for summer retreats off the beaten path, away from established resort areas where land prices had become prohibitive for all but the very wealthy. As summer people began to buy small acreage and to build, they were given the same welcome that full-time residents received.

Wilson Woody left his home in the North Carolina mountains in the early 1950s. He worked in Florida but returned home every chance he got—mostly for a few days, then later, as he gained more seniority in his job, for a few weeks and, more recently, for the whole summer. He owns his family land, and his wife, Estelle, who hails from the mountains of eastern Kentucky, loves the North Carolina hills almost as much as Wilson does. In recent years, their lives had become quite comfortable—their children were grown, and they had saved a little money—so Wilson and Estelle bought a recreational vehicle to drive to the mountains. They would park it on a little corner of the land, live in it for the summer, and plan for the time after Wilson's retirement when they could stay past the first frost, when they could settle back into those cold nights and warm friendships that they regarded as mountain winters. They had grown weary of the seasonless years in Florida and looked forward to a new life back home.

Wilson and Estelle finally got their dream. This time they drove up from Florida with both the recreational vehicle and the Buick packed to the brim, knowing that apple cider time would no longer signal a reluctant return to work.

The summer before, Wilson and Estelle had diligently searched want ads in the local papers until the right deal had finally come along on a two-year-old mobile home. Wilson and Estelle had looked at it and within two months had the site prepared and the home moved onto their land. The seventy-by-ten-foot mobile home had dwarfed the recreational vehicle, and by the end of the summer, they couldn't see how they had ever managed before in the cramped quarters of the RV.

The trailer weathered well over the winter, with no real damage from the snow, ice, and winds that sweep up the hollow in January. Wilson and Estelle arrived with new excitement and anticipation. Wilson's retirement party was in April, and by the middle of May he was home—really home, this time for good. The new mobile home represented to Wilson and Estelle a new freedom, stability, and continuity with Wilson's past.

Although Estelle loved the trailer—its new furnishings, the kitchen, and big windows—she still felt cramped. She had never lived in a trailer before, and it just felt too confining. Her head felt as her chest so often did with the recurring bronchial complications—a feeling of tightness, closeness, even of near-suffocation. From the start, she had urged for more room, more space. They had so many things, so much furniture, and so many friends. Estelle loved to entertain their friends and wondered where they would put them when they came to visit.

So, not long after they had settled in for the summer, Wilson and their Florida buddy Henry, whom they had lured up to North Carolina and who had finally bought a tract of land down the road, started studying how to expand the trailer. They cut a hole six feet wide in the back wall and during the summer added a trim, ten-by-twenty-eight-foot room onto the back of the trailer. They divided this room in two—a large main room, a kind of den that was entered from the living room, and a smaller pantry room on the end, accessed from both the den and the kitchen. Each room had its own exterior door, which, despite the cost, pleased Estelle, who needed to feel that she could get out in a hurry. By late August Henry had completely finished not only the exterior of the new structure but also all the final interior touches, including molding, carpeting, and lighting. The den matched the decor of the rest of the trailer so well that one would have thought it had been factory-made with the trailer.

One feature made the new addition a particularly special part of the home—the wood-heating stove. Wilson kept a plentiful supply of wood on hand and a good supply stored in the pantry, so he and Estelle, neither of whom had experienced cold weather in their years in Florida, could bask in the warmth if they wanted to. "There's no fire like a wood fire, no heat so penetrating as wood heat," they agreed.

More recently Wilson's health has been failing. He has thus become increasingly dependent upon his nephew and his sister for work around the place and has been increasingly reintegrated into the community.

Henry and his wife, Ruth, bought Wilson and Estelle's recreational vehicle and repeated the other couple's pattern of winter in Florida and summer in the mountains. For a while, they parked on Wilson and Estelle's land and spent their days on their newly acquired hillside, clearing brush and putting in fences, and by the end of the first summer, they had built a sturdy ten-by-ten-foot shop for storage of tools. After wintering in Florida, they returned in the early spring and

began building their house. Henry and Ruth worked well and
long together, putting up the neat brick house in a record four
months' time. By July, the house was finished, the carpeting
was laid, and new appliances installed; the yard had even
been landscaped, and the grass was ready for mowing. That
year they returned to Florida for only three months, as they
were anxious to be in their new mountain home.

Henry and Ruth, both in their late fifties, are not typical of
the tourists or summer people who frequent the mountains
from Florida. Henry is a skilled carpenter from a working-
class background. He and Ruth met and married in Illinois,
where they lived for ten years before following the building
boom to Florida. Henry's working-class background and
building experience stood him in good stead as he entered the
local "good old boys" network, and he got along far better at
first with men in the community than most flatlanders, who,
because of the wealth and status that afford them the luxury
of a second home in the mountains, usually find themselves
at a social distance from their primarily working-class neighbors. A natural talker, Henry related well to his rural neighbors, who found his stories and his brashness entertaining.
Ruth, like many mountain wives, disapproved of Henry's
drinking, so Henry, like many local men, drank away from
home, in a neighbor's garage or driveway or in his car.

While the 1960s were a time for "summer people," the
1970s saw the beginnings of another type of movement, as
younger families began to arrive with a back-to-the-land goal
for their lives. In many cases, they had a vision of an intimate
relationship with the bounteous mountain environment that
could be achieved through economic self-sufficiency and separation from mainstream society. They came seeking land
and space and wooded, well-watered, sparsely populated
mountain hillsides.

In many respects, these 1970s back-to-the-landers tended
to be products of the social changes taking place in the 1960s
on American college campuses and in the society as a whole
and were seeking refuge from the structures of American
mainstream society. They also hoped to create something
new, a new way of living and a new relationship to the phys-

ical environment. Some were artists and crafts people with products to sell in local shows and shops; others, with experience on the land, came from counterculture communities elsewhere to the lush, sparsely populated mountains where land was relatively inexpensive. But most were relatively fresh from academic and professional communities, having worked for a few years in the public sector to establish equity that enabled them to buy into the mountain environment.

From an upper-middle-class, southern family, Larry had graduated from college and spent four years in the navy. Linda grew up in the midwest and, after college, worked for an arts cooperative. They met in San Francisco. Larry says that, while he was in the navy, he decided that within two years of getting out he would be "sitting on top of a mountain somewhere."

Linda and Larry, and others like them, brought with them a vision of an idyllic experience with the natural world that economic self-sufficiency would bring. "Living off the land" became not simply a popular goal but a code word for a social movement that would mature as the decade wore on. For many families who came to the mountain communities in rural North Carolina, this vision was clear: economic self-sufficiency would allow one to reject and isolate oneself from the constraints, pressures, and unhealthy tensions of mainstream society and would provide the opportunity for spiritual growth, expanded consciousness, physical health, mental well-being, and creative self-expression, through the full appreciation and utilization of the beauty of the natural world.

Back-to-the-landers in the southern Appalachians in the 1970s were generally well educated, having started and usually finished an undergraduate degree, with a generous sprinkling of masters degrees and teaching certificates, and a few doctorates. From middle-class backgrounds, they had traveled fairly widely and had knowledge of urban life and political processes. Having made great changes in lifestyle in order to come to the mountains, they were well versed in counterculture philosophy and rhetoric.

Most early back-to-the-land families had a mountain "pat-

ron" who made the transition to the local community beara-
ble and, in fact, possible. The patron was usually a close
neighbor, landlord, or person from whom land had been purchased. The patron began the relationship by giving fresh
produce or other home-prepared gifts to the new residents
and became very rapidly the back-to-the-lander's primary
source of all conceivable types of information, ranging from
gardening, plumbing, household maintenance, and an assortment of services to community gossip. Since a vast amount of
knowledge of local people and, particularly, their skills and
expertise is commonplace in rural communities, the back-to-
the-landers had to rely on the help of their patron to function
effectively. The back-to-the-lander was likewise drawn into
the patron family's set of primary relationships.

Larry and Linda worked hard both to make a go of their
place and to get along with the neighbors. Besides J.B. and Iris,
who became like parents to them, they visited all up and
down the creek. They bought milk from Elmer and Helen
Giles, and every purchase meant a long visit. They traded
seed with John and Louise Blackwelder and gleaned much
useful information from Louise on planting by the signs and
old-timey seed strains and on herbal curing and folk medicine
from John, who had doctored neighbor children during long
winters when the snows made visits to a doctor impossible.
They made many friends in the community and participated
in the daily life, family cycles, and seasonal and personal
events of the community. They attended birthday parties,
wedding showers, and baby showers; they traded labor and
worked for neighbors; they shared meals, times of joy, and
times of sadness. They listened to community gossip, offering opinions and perspectives, and were the objects of community gossip; they were included in the intrigues of
courtship and pending elopements and learned the details of
family tensions and historical relationships. Their home,
though far off the main road, was always open to neighbors
who dropped in and who were never refused time to sit and
talk. Linda and Larry were gracious and friendly; the neighbors found them different yet entertaining, and their open-
ness invited neighborliness, even when it was not sought or

wanted. And always, Iris and J.B. were there to share food, knowledge, and time with them. J.B. plowed their garden, mowed their meadow, bulldozed their road, worked their bees, and did a hundred other acts of kindness to help them get along. Iris gave them food, helped can and freeze, and gave words of advice, encouragement, and counsel. Larry and Linda returned the many acts of kindness and neighborliness as best they could, but it was nearly impossible to begin to repay all of the favors. Instead they returned their friendship.

While privacy and private ownership of property were highly valued, work sharing, cooperative endeavors, and mutual aid were likewise important back-to-the-land goals. Basic to the vision was the ideal of making a living in the context of one's own home and by one's own hands—that is, making a living as part and parcel of making a life. This view necessitated a rejection of the notion that men and women were expected to leave home in order to make a living and a rejection of the importance of upward mobility as defined by urban industrial society. Back-to-the-landers thus basically rejected the professions toward which many of them, as products of middle-class homes, had been educated and in which some had been successful for a time, and the type of social communities in which many had been raised, in favor of less economically competitive, more labor-sharing relationships. The "living" toward which adherents of this philosophy strove was one adequate to make land payments, keep enough food on hand to eat well, keep a vehicle on the road, and provide a little extra for other basic necessities such as clothing and occasional entertainment or vacations.

Shelter was, of course, a central consideration, and an incredible array of imaginative endeavors was explored, tried, and implemented. Alternative dwellings incorporated existing structures, secondhand materials, timber cut from the owner's land, and shared labor.

Likewise, the formal structures of Western religion were discarded in favor of a range of nontraditional Western and non-Western religious philosophies. While spiritual relationships were valued among back-to-the-landers, formal church structure was abandoned in favor of notions of connectedness

with "natural" forces. Back-to-the-landers felt little affinity
with the small, family churches in the community.

After they bought into a community, back-to-the-landers
were sometimes approached, at least in the early part of the
decade, by neighbors with land to sell who would rather sell
to a "hippie" than subdivide and end up with more "Florida
people." Sale to developers or summer people was considered
to be less desirable because it often entailed a more dramatic
alteration of the environment and affront to the local
culture—summer houses were put where houses had never
been (on the ridge tops); muddy roads cut through fields and
woods; signs for "Chipmunk Hollow," "Robin Roost,"
"Chestnut Ridge," or "Laurel Vue" were erected in the middle of named places; fences limited traditional access of local
people to community land; and pole lights shone 365 nights a
year over houses rarely occupied. "Hippies" at least would
embrace and live on the land, and often the back-to-the-
landers had friends who were seeking to participate in the
same experience and were therefore interested in buying.

Although Larry and Linda participated in the life of the
community, their primary social ties lay elsewhere, with
those people who shared their values and experiences. Larry
wanted to write fiction, to find quiet times of solitude for
writing, and to enjoy communion with friends to consider philosophical points of view alien to the convictions of
his neighbors. Linda wanted artistic outlets and people
with whom to share her ideas and perspectives. Consequently, they had many guests who came to the mountains
and camped, partied with them, played music, and shared
their vision of a natural, creative life. Larry and Linda both
welcomed the summer invasions and dreaded the disrup-
tions. Most guests, as participants in mainstream economic
cycles, chose the hot summer weekends to vacation with
Larry and Linda in the cooler mountains. These visits meant
no work done in the garden or around the house, many meals
for Linda to prepare, and often the expense of buying added
food. At the same time, it meant both welcome release from
the sameness of the daily routine and also the pleasure of
partying, music, and sharing idyllic visions. On occasion,

guests would come to help work in exchange for their vacation in the mountain setting. Some friends did help paint the house, tend the garden, and finish several projects, but this work sharing was the exception rather than the rule.

A significant part of Larry and Linda's relationships with visiting outsiders was a shared vision of a counterculture community in the mountains. They were always looking for others who could buy land and move to the area. They were thus overjoyed when they could introduce Grant and Jenny to Joe, J.B.'s son-in-law, who had acquired from his wife's grandfather the large tract of land above and surrounding Larry and Linda's land. Grant and Jenny were professional people from the piedmont with two young children. They bought the hundred-acre tract with a dream of eventually moving onto the land, with Grant working from Rocky Creek. The large land payments they would have to make precluded their moving up very soon, although they envisioned building a house so that they could spend weekends on the land, and Jenny and the children could spend the summers, with Grant commuting to the piedmont as necessary.

Doug and Nancy Fields and their son, Nate, met Larry and Linda and the community through relatives in Brownsville. Originally from California, they had lived in Florida before following the route from Florida to the North Carolina mountains. They ended up in Brownsville because Nancy's brother and his wife had moved there, and they were introduced to Larry and Linda through the counterculture social network. They wanted only a small piece of land, which by 1977 was difficult to find and afford, so Larry and Linda introduced them to Grant, who sold them three acres. Nancy found work in Brownsville, and Doug began cutting timber for the house that he built, all the while looking for work. They became close to Iris and J.B. and to a few other local families.

As each new couple followed friends, acquaintances, or relatives to the mountains, they located their land through an established realtor, a local county store, a local land entrepreneur, or a friend's connections in the community. Back-to-the-landers often knew at least one counterculture family

through whom they were directed into the community, although they also were occasionally introduced through a
local health-food store, restaurant, or craft shop. They were
rapidly assimilated into the growing counterculture community through frequent social gatherings such as volleyball
games or parties. Even if they did not know any members of
the local counterculture community well, they were assisted
in every way possible during their settling-in period. A casual
meeting in a store in town or in a friend's home or a name
provided by a mutual friend gave the newcomer extensive
rights to ask for advice or help in finding land or housing or
even to be put up for a few days. They might camp on another
back-to-the-lander's property or stay in their home during the
transition. Assimilation of the newcomer was rapid because
the resident back-to-the-landers assumed that a decision to
settle locally implied a very specific set of shared values. As a
group, they were prepared for hardship and struggle. The
rhetoric and lifestyle were so extensively shared that formal
introductions and long periods of getting acquainted were
seldom needed before close helping and sharing relationships
were established.

The seeds of Larry and Linda's difficulty with and ultimate
departure from the community were sown in the increasing
complexity of their involvement with the Rocky Creek community. They had come to the community not seeking a
community, neighbors, or participation in the daily routines
of mountain life; instead, they wanted an idyllic sense of
solitude, a pristine existence in relationship to nature. They
had a vision—like others who followed them—of a type of
existence free from the bounds, rules, and norms of mainstream, or any, society, in communion with the "natural
world," where free expression of all sorts was possible. But as
Larry reflected on several occasions, the success of the sort of
venture they were seeking was ultimately dependent upon
their participation in the traditional community and upon
the many acts of kindness that neighbors would trouble
themselves to extend. Larry mused that he ought to write a
handbook for back-to-the-landers, emphasizing the importance of getting along with the neighbors. The very isolation

and natural beauty that made the mountains desirable for those seeking an alternative lifestyle also made getting along difficult and, at times, nearly impossible.

During the spring the garden needed turning in preparation for planting. Household maintenance and repair required tools and skills that back-to-the-landers had neither the resources nor the time to acquire. Cars needed repairs and spare parts as the dirt and gravel roads took their toll. Winter snows and spring floods rearranged gravel driveways, requiring bulldozer work. Survival during the spring, summer, and fall was comparatively easy, but winter was hard on Larry and Linda, as on others like them. Poorly insulated or uninsulated houses, wood heat and cookstoves and dwindling woodpiles, frozen water pipes, outdoor toilets, lack of jobs and money, impassable roads, and for some, lack of food, as well as winter flu and colds, loneliness, and boredom made life uncomfortable at best and, at times, tenuous. Those who survived the winter without abandoning their new locations for warmer climates or for friends with warm houses and good jobs in cities away from the mountains gradually learned, as did Larry and Linda, the necessity of getting along with the neighbors so that the neighbors could help them survive.

For Larry and Linda, the facts of mountain community life became quite clear. One became a neighbor by participating in the social life of the community, and in turn, neighborliness was linked with mutual aid. Survival was dependent on mutual aid, and aid was returned through neighborliness. Neighborliness precluded privacy and social isolation and laid one open to the social norms of the community.

Back-to-the-landers were committed to moderate acreage at first. The overwhelming majority wanted to acquire ten to fifteen acres. They often bought as much land as they could afford and after two or three years were ready to sell up to half of it. They were buying the potential for self- sufficiency and, equally important, for privacy and a controlled environment. They envisioned crops that were never planted with equipment that they could not afford, using time that was never available.

The first year on the land was both exhilarating and disastrous; the newcomers learned, on the one hand, that mountain living entails long, hard hours and, on the other, that not even a quarter of the intended projects would be accomplished. However, the rewards of any gardening attempts were greater than anticipated. The first winter overwhelmed them, as the house was poorly insulated at best, and the woodpile never was quite high enough. The second year yielded a newfound confidence and expertise, and they were able to relax about unfinished projects. Standards had been lowered as the reality of the requirements for subsistence living became clear. By the third year, the lifestyle itself began to be questioned in whispered tones that would become increasingly audible. Boredom was a problem; sameness was tedium; friends, who were similarly bored, were likewise boring. During the third to fifth year, some dramatic shifts were likely to occur. If a new job was not found that would open up a different set of social relationships, often with the town counterculture or establishment, and if the marriage had not dissolved, the likelihood of a move away increased dramatically. Strict commitment to the initial back-to-the-land ideal and plan had disappeared by the end of the fourth year.

Back-to-the-landers were committed to children. A few came with small children and many began having children during or after their first year—if their marriage lasted that period. Families were mandatory for this type of existence, and thus if the wife left (the husband rarely left), the husband found it almost impossible to carry on.

As back-to-the-landers established daily routines, a sexual division of labor began to emerge that was similar to that found in the traditional community. Men acquired skills and directed their energies toward building, wood collecting, and large-scale farming activities, although they also worked with planting and tending the garden, food storage, and other traditionally female work. They also began to participate in the local male gossip networks, gaining through the customary local means the information and assistance necessary for getting by. At the same time, responsibility for domestic areas became increasingly the domain of women, as did gardening, food preparation, and food storage, including drying, canning, and freezing. Information and skills to prepare food for storage was gained from local neighbor women as well as from other counterculture women.

The daily burden of survival thus became increasingly a female responsibility, and although female back-to-the-landers initially welcomed the flurry of productive activities, they quite often found themselves increasingly isolated from other companionship, increasingly overworked, and increasingly restricted in their activities. For these women, who had shared with their mates the larger vision, the fruits of their labor were more evident on a daily or weekly basis than were those of the men, who usually had planned on accomplishing much too much for the time, energy, and resources that they had available. Yet strains became evident in their relationship.

The financial burdens on the back-to-the-landers necessitated regular income sources, and eventually the wife of the household might find employment to support the family. More jobs, although low paying, were available to women in the mountain communities, and especially for women with college degrees. In addition, male labor was considered more valuable in reaching the back-to-the-land goal of economic self-sufficiency, since men were often involved in building and remodeling houses and outbuildings, fencing, cutting wood, and farming. The domestic and gardening activities of women, as in the traditional family, were thus fit into working women's busy schedules in the evenings and on weekends.

As the back-to-the-land movement gained momentum through the decade of the 1970s, the movement itself began to change. Those people like Larry and Linda who made their move during the early seventies were groundbreakers; as innovators, they had a more pristine, yet vague, formulation of the vision. Having not anticipated the problems that would arise and having no one to warn them or caution them to pragmatism, they were more idealistic than those who would follow. The vision was pure, new, and wholly theirs. Their move into the mountains pitted them against the natural elements and against the demands of a harsher way of life. During the bulk of their time on the land, at least during the first years, they were alone with their vision, their land, and the local community. They did not threaten the local community as much as the growing number of counterculture people did, and they were welcomed into local helping networks. As loners, they slipped into a dependence on the local mutual-aid networks; they survived their initial years by participating in the local community.

This participation, as well as the hardships of moving onto the land, forced an altered vision, a new pragmatism, and a certain cynicism about the back-to-the-land vision, about the local community, and in fact, about all community. As Larry said, "Where else is there to go?" Larry and Linda's experiences forced them to take a new look at their own values and a new look at society in general. Realizing that they could not escape society altogether, that the lifestyle they desired required an income, that subsistence living required hard work in not very creative ways, and that isolated rural living precluded certain types of cultural activities that the local economy could not support, they were forced to modify their vision and choose elements of the urban setting in which to participate.

As it matured during the 1970s, the back-to-the-land vision of life in the mountains had less room for the daily lives of the indigenous people who lived in the mountains. Of particular interest, however, were old farmers who possessed knowledge of traditional subsistence techniques, particularly since many of them remembered a time when self-sufficiency within the community was the norm. Implicit in the back-to-the-land philosophy was economic self-sufficiency, and earlier times in the mountains when self-sufficiency was the norm were idealized though usually poorly understood. The back-to-the-lander's guidebooks were the *Foxfire* books, *Mother Earth News*, and energy-efficient shelter and cosmic-consciousness books, which little prepared them for the social processes in the mountain communities.

By 1978 several back-to-the-landers in other communities in Linda and Larry's area had given up the difficult life and had found good jobs in Asheville, Charlotte, and other cities. The city had much to offer in the way of cultural stimulation, theater, entertainment, cultural diversity, quality schools, counterculture communities, jobs, and housing, particularly in comparison to the Rocky Creek area. After their second son, Scott, was born during the winter of 1979, Larry and Linda left the community for the city. They moved into a spacious apartment, and Linda reveled in the central heat. The school bus picked up Louis at the front door, (quite a change from the early-morning hikes down the long driveway in the cold and dark), and a variety of stores were within walking distance. Larry found work and Linda joined a theater group. Many of their friends were couples they had known in Rocky Creek, former back-to-the-landers who were buying and remodeling old houses available in downtown Asheville.

Although Grant and Jenny, after nine years, had still not built, they continued to have an annual party on their land and to spend occasional weekends camping there. As their lives became more complicated and took new turns, the probability that they would ever move permanently to the community became more remote.

For Doug and Nancy Fields, financial worries and their son's difficulty with school eventually drove them elsewhere. Doug could not find work, and Nancy's salary was low, typical of local standards. However, Nate was a precocious high school student who made no friends and was a social outcast. His difficulty with his peers as well as with his school principal led Doug and Nancy to explore job possibilities in Asheville. Doug quickly found an excellent job in Asheville, where they moved; after a while, Nancy too found a satisfying and lucrative job. Nate soon acquired a circle of friends and was happy in school. Doug and Nancy rented their Rocky Creek house to another newcomer, who worked for the Forest Service and who, with his wife and small child, "keep pretty much to themselves," according to Iris.

For Linda, despite her life in the city, Rocky Creek is still "home." She feels most comfortable there, she is attached to the land, and she values the good relationships with the neighbors. However, she cannot live there, at least for now. Linda and Larry say they left the community for three quite explicit reasons: cultural "deprivation," at least in terms of the kinds of cultural activities they wanted in order to feel fulfilled; economics—the lack of funds and interesting work; and the lack of privacy, that is, their inability to be isolated from the social processes of the local community. As part of the early wave, they were embroiled in the community, subject to the community's norms, and thus part of the total social fabric.

In the 1980s, a trickle of summer people and retirees continue to move into the rural mountain communities, as they have since the 1960s. Younger, full-time residents likewise continue in small numbers to move in, and a more diversified immigrant community has emerged. Early back-to-the-landers were motivated by a total commitment to "living off the land," while later immigrants have an altered vision and different goals, within the consistent goal of living on the land.

In describing this immigration as it occurred in the rural community called Shiloh in western North Carolina, John Stephenson outlines the following groups of new property owners:

> Some, of course, were speculators who did not live there and never intended to. They hoped simply to enjoy financial gain. Others had bought property to enjoy short holidays, sometimes renting out their otherwise unoccupied houses in order to help meet the mortgage payments. Others had built or bought homes to which to retire; some of them had reached retirement and lived in Shiloh year-round. The remaining category was also full-time residents; these were the year-round dwellers with intentions of permanent residence who came to work in the vicinity and find a better life for themselves and their families. They were typically of working and child-rearing ages. [1984:195]

Stephenson describes the "commodification" of the idea of place that has been a major factor in the movement of urbanites into rural communities; these newcomers' movement into the rural community "had to do with the fulfillment of a dream—not always the same dream but some kind of imagined improvement in the quality of life . . . . What they had bought was, both literally and figuratively, a place" (1984:195).

While back-to-the-landers of the early seventies sought escape from mainstream society, events of the decade brought about a felt awareness that people could not escape from national issues. Environmental concerns related to nuclear energy production, acid rain, pollution of aquifers, and chemical waste disposal forced a realization that the environment, even in otherwise isolated mountain places, was not immune to urban forces and that decisions made in Washington or Knoxville affected even the most remote North Carolina communities—the very land and water were not sacrosanct. While the end of the Vietnam era had yielded a population of young people seeking escape—some to the southern Appalachians—from the national political scene, these events of the mid-1970s brought home to back-to-the-landers the extent to which even isolated mountain communities are tied to mainstream society.

By the 1980s, a significant counterculture community existed in the rural mountains, one that was geographically dispersed yet ideologically unified. These later immigrants came seeking land and a life connected to the land—if not a living off the land. As immigrants made friends first with other counterculture families, they sought out and nurtured significant participation in the growing counterculture community. Although the back-to-the-land vision was still in place, it was but one part of a mosaic of new insights developed as the result of economic and cultural forces in the society as a whole.

The existence of the counterculture community meant that less reliance on, or even consideration of, the local community was necessary. The close ties that had developed between the first immigrants and local people were no longer so important. A counterculture network had grown and was populated by individuals with varieties of skills, so that services needed could be found within the new community itself. The existence of a larger back-to-the-land community meant that winter boredom—cabin fever—could be alleviated within the newer community, and ties with the indigenous community were even less important.

The rapid increase in land speculation in general in the mountains, beginning during the later sixties, also had a major impact on the nature of the back-to-the-land movement. Larry and Linda were among the few who were able to buy land at rock-bottom prices and thus be relatively free of stable sources of income. Speculation by recreation and second-home developers and resource and energy industries, accelerated by nationwide inflation, began to raise the price of even isolated tracts of land far beyond what ordinary purchasers could afford. Thus those people who sought a life on the land had to have greater economic resources at hand and greater assurance of stable incomes with which to make their land payments. The local and national economic mood required a greater sense of economic pragmatism. The counterculture community thus had to modify its self-image to include a stable job, regular hours, work for a variety of agencies, dress appropriate to the position, more time away from home, and more participation in town and institutional life—in other words, it had to modify its ideal of self-sufficiency.

Public work meant less time on the land to pursue the self-sufficient ideal. It also meant greater cash flow and the possibility or necessity of buying items that earlier back-to-the-landers would have either grown or done without. The later immigrants lived a life more consistent with the middle-class families from which they had come than did the earlier participants. They could afford moderate wines, good sound systems, color televisions, an occasional steak (for the non-vegetarians), good coffee, a bottle of Scotch on hand, and a new Rototiller.

Tom and Sarah bought their house and thirty acres of pasture and woodlot and moved into Grassy Fork in 1977, after Sarah had gotten a teaching job in the county school system. Tom had a job in town, where they had lived for three years; in 1978, he quit his job in order to farm. While Tom had little knowledge of farming, he entered his work wholeheartedly and enthusiastically, relying heavily on his farming neighbors for advice. He developed an especially close relationship with an elderly neighbor, a successful full-time farmer with whom he traded labor, time, friendship, and gossip. Sarah continued to teach and became, like most teachers, a well-respected community member. While Tom and Sarah socialize primarily with other immigrants from urban areas, they are well integrated into the traditional Grassy Fork community.

In some areas, the movement of newcomers into the community, tolerated and even enjoyed by most people during times of plenty, was a convenient scapegoat for tensions during the economically lean early 1980s. In Rocky Creek, a skirmish arose between an immigrant couple and their indigenous neighbor over property lines and access roads. Threats were uttered and passed along through the gossip networks, fences were cut, bulldozers became the weapons, and a gun was displayed on one occasion. As the dispute developed, old resentments between neighbors surfaced, to be sparked and fueled by new alignments fostered by the influx of outsiders. Neighbors took sides, with their indigenous neighbor or with the newcomer, following traditional alliances.

Such overt displays were rare, however. As in the case of Shiloh, "whether new divisions within the community will erupt into overt conflict which tears apart the fragile structures of daily life remains to be seen. The transformation in Shiloh has been peaceable, but latent divisiveness remains a subliminal threat to community vitality. Presently, it exists at the level of mutually understood—and so far amiable—hypocrisy. This is partly because what resistance the natives feel is kept under control by a stronger ethic which prizes courtesy and the maintenance of smooth social relationships at almost all costs. There is also an almost total absence in this community of experience with organizational forms through which to mobilize resistance" (Stephenson 1984: 199).

As the decade of the 1970s came to a close, the back-to-the-land movement had made a significant and complex impact on the local social fabric. It dramatized and symbolized the changes in the nation as a whole that hurled the community into the national economic events. Increased land speculation and purchase by outsiders resulted in skyrocketing land prices and thus the decreasing availability of land for local use, as rising taxes became an increasing burden when weighed against the stability of agricultural income and as local young families were thus systematically excluded from the land market. Likewise, sale of land to outsiders created uneasiness as land became lost to the community of neighbors. Loss of local control of land meant loss of local participants in the social process, and this loss threatened the very basis of community.

The back-to-the-land movement had initially thrust the newcomers into the local social system, and the physical and economic environment had necessitated their participation in local community. However, as the decade wore on, as more young families moved into the mountains and as the economy shifted, a counterculture community began to evolve and, as it grew, could become increasingly independent of the traditional social system. Instead, a parallel social system developed that meshed with the traditional system on occasion, clashed at other times, but basically flowed along independently. While traditional community was associated with place, shared history, shared experiences, and mutual aid, the counterculture community was defined by shared vision, philosophy, and lifestyle; it cut across geographical boundaries and brought counterculture people from distant locales together, excluding and at times disrupting local patterns.

John Stephenson, in a comparable situation, describes the relationship between Shiloh natives and newcomers as generally "one of mutual tolerance, a keeping of distance, a muted disdain. Most of the newcomers expressed to me the feeling that they were well-accepted by the natives, but they admitted that they rarely associated with them except in public places such as the stores and in meetings. They had ideas about local culture which were not especially complimentary" (1984:197).

At times tension pervaded the attitude of the local community to the counterculture community. On the one hand, local people wanted their relationships with neighbors—of whatever origin—to follow traditional time-tested patterns. That is, they wanted neighbors simply to be neighbors. Neighbors share resources, knowledge, and culture: neighbors understand and respect, whether or not they follow community norms. They expected friendship and sharing, particularly since counterculture folks were indeed curious and interesting. The experiences and diversity they brought with them made them appealing and entertaining, and their insights—though frequently naive—were often useful or at least provocative. They provided spice of life. Furthermore, they had labor and time to share in traditional ways.

On the other hand, the counterculture folks were a convenient scapegoat for local tensions, as they were in truth representative of economic changes in the nation that were tearing at the local social fabric. They represented the unsettling cultural changes as children were exposed to drug use in public schools, women moved into the public labor force, unemployment rose, and the economy placed greater strain on the family.

As Stephenson suggests for Shiloh, "My impression is that the newcomers may now have a stronger sense of place than do the natives, who are uncertain what is happening to their place." One Shiloh native suggests, " 'You've got to have progress, but after you reach a point, you lose what you had and you can't get it back' " (1984:198).

Chapter Six

COMMUNITY: PAST PRESENT, AND FUTURE

THURSDAY AFTERNOON Gennifer left work, picked up her daughter at the day-care center, and stopped by the supermarket for a supply of items for the weekend. Too tired really to think what they needed to get through the next week and silently chastising herself for not having taken a few moments during the morning's rush to plan the week's meals and make a grocery list, she hurried through the store, picking up the milk, bread, and eggs that she knew they needed, all the while trying to keep the jubilant three-year-old moving in the right direction and just out of reach of the loaded supermarket shelves.

Gennifer did most of her grocery shopping in the supermarket in town, relying on George Wilson's neighborhood store for forgotten milk, eggs, or flour. She liked to visit in George's store and to support the local business with purchases, but the prices were higher than those in the chain stores in town. Sometimes Gennifer bought gas, food items, chicken feed, or an occasional tool at George's store, particularly near the end of the month when George would "put it on the tab"; George never seemed concerned about anyone's mounting bills. He would take food stamps and also cash paychecks, personal checks, or two-party checks, something that bigger stores in town wouldn't always do. Some neighbors bought most of their groceries at George's, particularly those who didn't have transportation. They would catch a ride with a neighbor or walk the short distance from their home and then either walk back home or get a ride.

George's store, a focus for daily community activity, is

open Monday through Saturday. Before dawn fully breaks in the morning, neighbors meet at George's to leave their cars and pool rides for the long drive to work in town. When George comes across the hill from his own house nearby to open up about seven, a neighbor or two are often waiting to get a few dollars' worth of gas, a little air in a low tire, a soft drink, a sweet roll, or a cup of coffee when George plugs in the pot. The television comes on, and men and women on their way to work or returning from feeding cattle pull up a crate and watch a few moments of "Good Morning America" over coffee and talk about weather, crops, community or national news, upcoming elections, and people passing through. Truckloads and carloads of men on their way to work stop to buy crackers and cans of pork and beans, sardines, or sausages and a soda for later lunch breaks. A slow but steady stream of neighbors and deliverymen come and go throughout the day, some pausing for a short chat and some making inquiries about neighbors or passing along the latest information about old folks in the hospital, trips out of town, sick cattle, crop fertilizers, local politics, and new babies.

George's wife, Sarah, comes in later in the morning to help tend the store or to relieve George for other work at home. Their daughter Jackie got off the school bus at the store almost every school day and spent the rest of the afternoon helping her parents in the store or visiting with friends and neighbors who dropped in. She is married now and living up the road in their new trailer on land her parents have given them. Yet she still works part-time in the store, helping out around her own part-time job.

George inherited the store from his father, who has passed away, and the new, corrugated-steel building with its large, asphalt parking lot, well illuminated by the giant EXXON sign, stands in marked contrast to the old, weathered, wooden building across the road that served the community for many years. Dora Hicks remembers working all through the summer of 1938, hoeing corn in neighbors' fields and earning enough money to buy the silk, at $1.25 a yard, for her wedding dress. The old store now is used for storage. Beyond the old building, on the hill across the road, George's brother lives with his family. Across from the store and down a hundred yards, George's son and his family live in their mobile home. George's brother and son and their families are in and out of the store for a visit or loaf of bread and can be counted on to step in and help a waiting customer when George or Sarah are busy hauling feed in the back room, looking for a pipe fitting, or pumping gas.

The Wilsons have lived their family life for two generations in the center of the community and well in the public view. Daughter Jackie had courted in the parking lot, leaning up against some boy's '72 Ford to discuss matters of high significance to young teenagers; she had studied her homework in a chair next to the shelves laden with auto parts; she and her Dad had studied tree data and crop charts spread over the counter between the cash register and the adding machine. She had learned to handle the occasional drunk who had come as far as the store but who was too tipsy to make it home. She would joke with him and find him a ride home with someone going that way. People noticed the small diamond on her finger when she began to ring up their purchases and shared in the excitement of her engagement and wedding plans.

Neighbors drop in on the way home from work for a loaf of bread and a few moments' conversation. Men working in the community take midmorning, lunch, or midafternoon soda, snack, and gossip breaks. Local auctions, bake sales, yard sales, revivals, and school fund-raising events are advertised in the store's windows and doors, and George and Sarah always know the details. The local volunteer fire department meets every Tuesday night at the store, and local men gather to discuss fire-department needs, as well as the widest range of local events.

THE MYTHIC PAST

The rural southern mountain community is of course, a geographical entity—an area of several square miles with definable natural boundaries.[1] Yet it is also an ideological entity—a body of individuals whose members are linked by kinship relations, historical events, and the requirements of making a living. "Independence" and "egalitarianism" are elements in this ideological system, and both values may usefully be viewed as myths that help sustain and define community. Myth refers to a story or an idea, the reality of which is assumed though unverifiable. Thus independence and egalitarianism are unattainable ideals believed to have existed in the historical past of the community, although this point can't be proven.

The myth of independence is that of the independent individual, one who is wholly self-sufficient economically, psychologically, and socially. This ideal, of course, is unattainable. The myth of independence demonstrates "the past made present and perfect" (Warner 1959:156). This myth creates the image of the self-sufficient individual who is honest and predictable, diligent, adaptable to varying circumstances, strong in defense of worthy goals, and generally worthwhile or honorable. The independent individual feels no need to explain or to account to anyone for actions, and the only reason for action is that one "took a notion." The independent individual is one to whom no one can give orders and, in particular, one whom no one will tell what he can or cannot do with his land. This myth is "individuating" in that it stresses the distinctiveness and autonomy of the individual.[2]

Egalitarianism, the second myth, is most frequently echoed in the expression "We're all just plain mountain folks." In one sense this statement may be an apology to the outsider for any difference in the standard of living between members of the community and American middle-class society in general; but more important, it is a way of articulating both the conceptual equality and the distinctiveness of those people who make up the community. Members of the rural mountain community see themselves as an entity significantly distinct from American society. They refer to their home region as "this country," meaning only the mountain area and not the nation as a whole. In this sense, egalitarianism becomes an "integrating" idea, for it provides the format through which shared beliefs are expressed and unity is achieved.

A set of beliefs results from many historical influences and events. Paradoxically, it is composed, at least in part, of selective remembrances and selective interpretations by the believers of these same historical influences and events. Furthermore "history" is interpreted in particular ways so that it becomes consistent with present beliefs (these beliefs, of course, being attributable in form and function to historical influences in numerous ways). Likewise, the beliefs in independence and egalitarianism in the mountain community have implications in social organization and interaction but are the result of, and are reflected in, the selective interpretation of history. History may thus be considered a myth, in a broad sense of the term, and a myth is a social "charter" that functions to reinforce social organization and interaction. History thus provides a "mythic charter" of community, since history may be interpreted selectively to justify existing beliefs.[3] As Stephenson suggests, with reference to the Shiloh community, "The past is more a reinforcing myth, a palliative for the present" (1968:106).

APPALACHIAN HISTORIES

Three kinds of popular histories are available on the Appalachian region: regional surveys, local histories, and oral histories. The first are called regional surveys because one finds in these works statements about the Appalachian region as a whole, rather than detailed analysis of specific locales.[4] Furthermore, one finds within this group three quite different impressions of the motivation and character of the first settlers. These produce very different interpretations of the history of the region. The first interpretation assumed that Appalachia was settled by noble Scotch-Irishmen (or "pure Anglo-Saxon") seeking freedom from tyranny. With axe, long rifle, and bear knife, they tackled the mighty wilderness in all its glory and trial and succeeded in defying the hostile forces of nature with unyielding devotion and courage. I call this interpretation the "Daniel Boone" approach.

Advocates of this approach often appeal to the Mecklenburg Declaration of Independence and to the Battle of King's
Mountain during the American Revolution as typifying the
spirit of freedom and democracy that inspired the ancestors
of the modern mountain people. Kephart, for example, states
with regard to the history of the Appalachian region: "Then
came the Revolution. The backwoodsmen were loyal to the
New American Government—loyal to a man. They not only
fought off the Indians from the rear, but sent many of their
incomparable riflemen to fight at the front as well. . . . They
carried the day at Saratoga, the Cowpens and King's Mountain. From the beginning to the end of the war, they were
Washington's favorite troops" (1913:152).

Another example of this approach may be found in John C.
Campbell's excellent work on the southern mountains.
Campbell provided the most extensive analysis of origins of
the mountain population, rejecting, for the most part, all
conjectures that lumped the population into one social, eth-
nic, economic, or personality category. Yet he too fell into the
trap of generalization on occasion, noting, for example:

Heredity and environment have conspired to make [the
Highlander] an extreme individualist. In his veins there
still runs strong the blood of those indomitable fore-
bearers who dared to leave the limitations of the known
and fare forth into the unknown spaces of a free land . . .
generation by generation, facing alone the dangers and
the hardships of the wilderness, they learned the ways of
freedom. From among them in the Carolina foothills
came, May 21, 1775, the first Declaration of Indepen
dence, whereby "we the citizens of Mecklenburg County," so ran the document, "abjure all political
connection, contract, or association with that nation
who have wantonly trampled on our rights and liber-
ties," and "do hereby declare ourselves a free and independent people." [1921:91]

Rural western North Carolinians know and most readily
identify with this approach to history and origins. Although

the Mecklenburg Declaration of Independence and the Battle of King's Mountain are significant events in the community's conceptual history, both occurred before settlement had developed very far—if it had begun at all. Furthermore, a history of one family in the Rocky Creek community suggests that the first permanent settler in the community was the son of a Tory who moved to the region to escape persecution in piedmont North Carolina for his father's Revolutionary War activities. In Plum Creek early settlers were Germans who immigrated from Piedmont North Carolina in the early nineteenth century.

Taking an entirely opposite view, the second interpretation of the founding fathers of the present society assumes that they were social misfits—political rejects who were to become isolated and highly inbred. One of the earliest statements of this argument was by Fiske, who in 1897 claimed that the settlers of North Carolina and of the southern mountains were "the shiftless people who could not make a place for themselves in Virginia society, including many of the 'mean whites' " (1897:31).[5] Noting that not all the mountain population is descended from this "degraded white humanity" or these "crackers," Fiske states that this group "furnished a nucleus about which various wrecks of decayed and broken-down humanity from many quarters were gradually gathered" (1897:321).

Allegedly because of their ignorance of proper ecological practices in mountain farming and because of the potential ruthlessness of sweet-talking northern establishment capitalists, the mountaineers were to become inheritors of barren wastelands and denizens of welfare rolls. A more recent example of this approach to history may be found in Caudill's otherwise powerful analysis of several coal-producing regions in Appalachia: "For many decades there flowed from Merry England to the piney coasts of Georgia, Virginia and the Carolinas a raggle-taggle of humanity. . . . It is apparent that such human refuse, dumped on a strange shore in the keeping of a few hundred merciless planters, was incapable of developing the kind of stable society under construction in the Puritan North. . . . Instead . . . we must start with the cynical, the penniless, the resentful and the angry" (1963:5-6). This perspective is developed to an absurd degree in his undocumented 1976 work, *A Darkness at Dawn.* Although few people in the rural communities were familiar with this explanation of their origins, those who could comment regarded it as totally inaccurate, inapplicable to the settlement of western North Carolina, or simply slanderous.

The third approach reflects the new identity struggle that has emerged in the last half decade, particularly in reaction to the "colonizing" of the mountains by industrial interests outside the region[6] and to the effects of the degrading and demoralizing comic figure of the "hillbilly" portrayed in such television shows as the "Beverly Hillbillies" and "Hee Haw," comic strips such as "Li'l Abner" and "Snuffy Smith," and movies such as James Dickey's *Deliverance* (1972).[7] Important to these analyses of history are, for example, the Unionist sympathies held by mountain people during the Civil War, mountain abolitionist sentiments, and the heroes of the unionizing struggles in mountain industries, notably the coal industry. Examples of this approach may be found in West (n.d.), Whisnant (1973), Parton (1925), and Greene (1971). Although many mountain residents are highly critical of the hillbilly stereotype, the exploitation of mountain resources by eastern and northern "foreigners," and the differential treatment of mountain and nonmountain portions of the state by both state and federal governments, the fact remains that Rocky Creek, Plum Tree, and Grassy Fork (and the counties in which they lie) allied with the Confederacy during the Civil War; there were slaves in each county; western North Carolina has no coal; and the three communities have seen only the beginnings of large-scale industrial development. The residents thus have little reason at present for subscribing to this view of history.

The second type of history is the local history, usually written by local historians. In two communities, the historians were university-educated persons closely associated with the public school systems, local governments, and the middle- and upper-class town leaders and organizations. The histories are overt attempts to demonstrate the middle-class-ness of the present population and the heroics of the past. As an example, one such local history includes the following qualification: "The feature writer[s] have refused, or at least have failed, to see the progress that has been made in these regions, and most of all they have failed to understand that an intelligent planning and leadership have been present quite as much as in the better known regions. . . . [The people] have always shown a keen interest in state and national affairs . . . progress was made in that section under great handicaps; . . . it was populated by a respectable class of people, alert, hard-working, intelligent, and ambitious; . . . and it was possessed of high principles of democracy and nationalism" (Deyton 1947:423). Similarly, the history of another mountain county includes a section entitled "Sketches of Prominent Families," besides the following analysis:

> The game was driven into the intervening mountains, and only the bravest and the hardiest of the frontiersmen of the borders followed it and remained after it had been exterminated . . . the true pioneers dwelt afar in trackless mountains, in hunting camps and caverns, from which they watched their traps and hunted deer, bear and turkeys . . . the hunters waxed stronger and braver, and their descendants still people the mountain regions of the South. . . . Kephart puts it in another form only when he says (p. 307), "The nature of the mountaineer demands that he have solitude for the unhampered growth of his personality, wing-room for his eagle heart." As another said of the Argonauts, "The cowards never started, and the weaklings died on the way." [Arthur 1915:8]

Although many residents of these two communities knew that the local histories existed, few were familiar with the specific content. Of most interest, though, to those who knew of these documents was mention of their own ancestors' names; individuals were concerned with their own roots in the community, more than with specific historical events.

The third type of history is oral history, the verbal account of the past as told by individual members of the community. The content of oral history is usually the association of particular ancestors with specific deeds and misdeeds in the past. In the community, oral history accounts assume a certain social timelessness within three loosely defined categories of objective time: first the settlement period, also known as the "old days," the "old timey" period, or the "pioneer days," beginning around the late eighteenth century and continuing until the Civil War; next, the Civil War period; and last, recent history, dating from the end of the Civil War to the present. The belief underlying oral history is that the founders of the mountain community struggled against great obstacles to carve out homesites and garden plots and to survive. Significant are the notions of the isolation and trials these people faced and the fierce determination and spirit of independence they exhibited.

Culture heroes of the first period are men like Daniel Boone and Abraham Lincoln. Although political alliances during the Civil War were mixed (as they are now), Lincoln is a national hero divorced from the Civil War. Lincoln has been called "the symbolic culmination of America," and for rural Appalachia, as well as for urban America, he is both an egalitarian symbol of "the common man" and the "new democracy" and a symbol of the "rags-to-riches motif" of the American success story (Warner 1959:271-72). Charles Phillips, a widower in his eighties, went so far as to compare the trials he faced in his own upbringing in Rocky Creek to those of Lincoln:

> I decided I'd do like Abe Lincoln. Now I came up as hard as Abe Lincoln did; I guess you read all about Abe Lincoln; how poor his father was, and how he got his education. Why, I can see Abe set before the fire—didn't have no lamps or nothin' in his day, and if he did I ain't heard of 'em. He'd set by the fire and lean up against the chimney, and he had him an old shovel, and he'd take a far coal, and he'd figurin', and he'd get that all covered up, and he'd take an old rag and he'd wipe that all off and then he'd try it over. Abe Lincoln was a smart man. The

south didn't treat him right. They killed him. Right
when they needed him the worst. They needed him the
worst right then.

Egalitarianism is a function of rootedness in the community and the community's collective representation of its
own historical mythic charter. History in this sense is a
leveling mechanism, because common origins and common
motivation for migration and settlement in the region, as
well as common environmental difficulties that everyone
faced and that had no easy or financially accessible solutions,
equalized the status and alternatives of residents.

The idea that "we've been here forever" (the "we" being
predominantly of Scotch-Irish and German descent) is important. The unity and equality of residents is reinforced
through collective recognition of common and well-estab-
lished roots. Ideas on motivation for settlement are thus
dominated by the desire for escape from tyranny and oppression, for democratic freedom, for democratic equality, and for
representation, recognition, and economic alternatives for
the common people.

The second category of objective time is the Civil War
period, a short time period chronologically but of great social
significance, filled with strife and destruction. The Civil War
was particularly traumatic in Rocky Creek, as Yancey County and the adjoining county, Mitchell, took opposite sides
during the war, and fighting and raiding occurred frequently.
In each community, however, stories are told of how women
and children faced the threats of marauders, how clothing
and food were hidden, how crops were made, and how families survived the war years often without men in the households.

The end of the war left Yancy and Mitchell counties torn
by political strife, the vestiges of which are still visible in
local sentiments toward the other county and in the respec-
tive political party alignments. Many old residents in each
community strongly associate their present party affiliation
with that of ancestors who fought in, were killed in, or were
ravaged by, the Civil War.

The third period of oral history is the "modern period," encompassing all events since the Civil War and continuing to the recent past. This period is one of progress and development, including the coming of paved roads, automobiles, and electricity; depopulation resulting from migration to industrial centers; and the beginnings of occupational specialization. Three types of events are significant in this period. First are technological changes and particular ancestors' roles in helping to bring about these changes. Many of the old people vividly remember how they, and relatives whom they had known, coped with the problem of subsistence before modernization. They recalled how some people were instigators of progress through the introduction of such things as the portable sawmill, the truck, and electric lights. In particular, they recalled that, before innovation, people were generally more self-reliant in subsistence and entertainment but that the community as a whole was more cohesive.

The second type of event is the early social gathering, such as quiltings and square dances, which middle-aged and elderly people remember with a great sense of nostalgia. Middle-aged residents remember the community as an economically and socially centralized place, augmented by local schools, stores, a post office, or a site where the train could be flagged down. This picture existed before consolidation of schools and of postal facilities, before the supermarkets, and before industry began to draw people away from the community.

The third type of event includes stories of unusual, deviant, antisocial, or otherwise exceptional and, thus, interesting and well-known events in the past of particular individuals, such as pranks, fights, cases of abandonment, and sexual deviance. These events were related for a variety of reasons, involving explanations for the present behavior of individuals based on past behavior or experiences, examples of past individual heroics or deviance in the face of stress, or simply entertainment or amusement through humor or the bizarre.

Shared recent history reinforces the unity of community experience. Collective history is shaped both by environmen-

tal crises such as especially severe winters, bad flooding, and
crop failures and by economic fluctuations such as the timber
boom and bust, the mineral boom and bust, and the "Great
Migration" to urban centers and its accompanying frustrations.

Times of individual, familial, and communitywide crisis
have accentuated the need for both independence and cooperation. The Great Depression affected southern Appalachia, as
it did the nation as a whole. Yet for the rural community this
was a time when "nobody starved." Most people did without
new goods but were able to weather the financial disaster by
relying on traditional subsistence techniques. As one man
said, "We couldn't buy no new things like shoes or trousers;
we just kept repairing what we had, but we didn't go hungry."
Furthermore, "people helped each other more."

Personal and familial crises were, and are, shared by wide
networks within the community. A subsistence farmer in
Rocky Creek sold four thousand dollars' worth of tobacco to
try to defray the cost of his deceased son's hospital bills,
accrued during a terminal illness. It is common knowledge
that money came from all over "the country" to help defray
the costs. All donations were anonymous since, as one friend
said, "He would have tried to pay back the money if he had
known where it came from." Funerals and illnesses are borne
by wide networks of people who contribute food, money, and
other types of assistance to people in the crisis situation.
Collective history shares the births, deaths, marriages,
crises, joys, embarrassments, and disgraces of community
families and reinforces the ties of mutual dependence among
residents.

People thus identify with two levels of history: collective
history and individual history. On the first level, community
or collective history associates the community in general
with the first type of regional history and with local history
to some degree. At this level lies the "mythic charter" of the
community. Briefly, the myth may be outlined as follows: the
original settlers in the community, the ancestors of the pres-
ent-day population, migrated from Europe, primarily from
Scotland, Ireland, and/or Germany to the Appalachian

Mountains. They came seeking escape from tyranny and desiring to establish a new type of life in freedom on a new frontier. They believed in independence from European powers, as demonstrated by the Mecklenberg Declaration of Independence, and the importance of a new democracy, as witnessed by heroic fighting to defeat the British in the American Revolution. At the same time they dealt quite successfully with the hostile environment. Though the environment was severe, those who were independent and clever—the true mountain people—succeeded in coping with the hostile factors, so that they could partake of the bounty and beauty of the mountain environment. The society's relationship to the environment is an ambivalent one, as expressed in the statement, "This is God's country, 'cause the devil wouldn't have it." It is a place of wondrous beauty but difficult terrain, and subsistence demands great toil, strength of character, independent action, self-sufficiency, and cooperation.

The second level of history with which people identify is individual history, summarized by a sense of rootedness in the community and land of family members, regardless of the actual settlement dates. Thus community members value the statement "We've been here forever." When queried as to country of origin, the informants' response is usually, "I reckon we're Scotch-Irish [German]."[8] Hence independence becomes an inheritable trait, dependent on "rootedness." Rootedness itself, however, symbolizes both unity and equality of community members by virtue of similar ancestry and common kinship origins.

SOCIAL ORGANIZATION

Collective history and the "mythic charter" of the community relate the ideal independence of the present community to the historical experience of settlement, subsistence, and survival. Included in the collective history of the community, however, are two somewhat different interpretations of the ideal of independence. First, independence means freedom from institutional or organized tyranny. This type of independence is interpreted as the prime reason for settlement in the mountains and is offered as the explanation for such phenomena as mountain sentiments against the British during the American Revolution, later against governmental taxation, and now against governmental taxation and environmental controls.

Second, independence suggests self-sufficiency in an inhospitable environment—the ideal independence of the individual member of society, valued because survival was historically dependent upon it. The ideology of independence thus equates the ideal independence of the individual to the ideal state of adulthood, as opposed to that of childhood dependence. Independence is one important attribute of adulthood and is conceived more specifically as the capability of the individual adult to participate fully in all aspects of social and economic interaction, to be fully responsible and accountable for decisions and actions, and to be self-sufficient in coping with the environment.

Both parts of this conceptual system support marriage, since marriage is the ritual act or confirmatory rite that marks the distinction between the dependent and the independent individual and that creates the new nuclear family unit. The transition of the individual from the category of dependent child to independent adult occurs through marriage; although sometimes sudden and dramatic, marriage marks the community's acceptance of the new nuclear unit on an equal basis with other such units. Despite the reality of extended-family cooperation, the nuclear family, as the primary unit of production and consumption, is ideally independent of control from neighbor and kin.[9] Stephenson discusses mountain "individualism" as a "cultural doctrine," and I would extend his description to apply to the community view of the nuclear family. He states: "Independence, in this sense, means minding one's own business. This is a dictum more honored in the breach than in the observance—it is expected that a person will learn as much as he can about everyone else, but only so long as he does not misuse his knowledge. Minding one's business is in turn a way of preserving relationships and achieving harmony. It is another way of saying "Don't tell me what to do!" (1968:104). Thus when the term "independent" is used in the context of the nuclear family, no personality characteristics applicable to the individual per se are implied. Rather, the ideal autonomy and separateness of the self-contained subsistence unit is implied, particularly with respect to the view of this unit by the total community.

Independence, then, means "minding one's own business" or not meddling in other people's business and, at the same time, expecting to be left alone in managing one's own affairs. This concept is expressed most frequently in the simple phrase "Ain't nobody gonna tell me what to do." Thus the personal affairs of a particular individual or family may be well known and thoroughly discussed by friends, relatives, and strangers, but rarely would these same people overtly attempt to influence the decisions of the individual or family in a particular way. Unsolicited advice is not only unwelcome but it is rarely offered. When advice is requested, it is given with reservations and qualifications, such as: "It ain't none of my business, but . . .," followed by some relevant experience from the advice giver's own personal history from which some moral may be elicited. Likewise, discussions of particular individuals within gossip networks involve a straightforward telling of the events, prefaced by, "It ain't none of my business, but . . .," followed by, "If I was so-and-so I surely would [do the following]." The concluding opinions and evaluations are further qualified by, "I know it ain't none of my business, but I surely do hate to see so-and-so [suffer/be treated/treat him or her] that-a-way."

In sum, explanations for the existence and persistence of the myths of independence and egalitarianism lie in the social and economic matrix of the community's past and present. Community interaction is molded by the historic demands of a subsistence-oriented economy and by the effects of economic and social isolation in a relatively harsh terrain. The history of the region is dominated by factors that demanded that families by as self-sufficient as possible, yet cooperative, in order to survive. Equality provides the mechanism for cooperation in reciprocal relationships. To a great extent these economic conditions still influence relations among residents, despite the recent predominance of wage-labor employment. A fragile agricultural economy and public-work instability are dominant factors in the community's economy.

THE IDEOLOGICAL PRESENT

Community homogeneity is expressed in terms of the community's collective representation of its own historical mythic charter, involving notions of common ancestry, kinship, shared experience, and rootedness in place. Egalitarianism, or the equality of community members, and the inclusion of residents in the general social category of "most folks," are based on the concept of "worth." Worth, or the lack of it, is the measure of the individual in the community and is the most important factor from which community homogeneity is derived.

Worth is a term rarely used in a positive sense; the negative condition "worthlessness" is frequently expressed.[10] For example, "He ain't worth the bullet it'd take to kill him, or he'd a been dead years ago"; "that worthless old woman"; "he ain't worth shit"; and "he ain't worth a pinch of dried owl shit."[11] "Most folks," or people of worth, are responsible for their actions, are rational in their decisions, and have common sense. Common sense is an important quality of worth and is an innate quality that, if developed and used by the individual, motivates the individual to rational action. Worth is thus assumed to exist in people because they are people. Worth is a natural quality of adults, both male and female.

Young children have worth, and though they may act foolishly, irrationally, or in a worthless manner, it is not because of their own lack of worth but because of their parents' irresponsibility. Parents are responsible for the actions of their children; children must be taught self-control and responsibility if they are to "act right." Parents therefore may have indirect effects on the worth or lack of worth of adults. Worthless parents may produce children who become worthless adults who "don't know no better." However, children of worthless parents are not automatically categorized as worthless. All children, legitimate or not, or born of worthless parents or not, have the potential for worth and are not excluded by virtue of birth status or parentage. Each person demonstrates his or her own worth or lack thereof, and worthless parents may produce children of worth. The worthless "whoring" woman in the community who had illegitimate children by different men produced children of worth.

Although common sense is an important quality of worth, one may act as if one had "no sense" or "no common sense" and not by that fact alone be considered worthless. Lacking common sense, one is considered foolish or simply a fool. T.R. Campbell has no common sense. T.R. and his wife, Sally, and their two small children live on part of T.R.'s parents' 135 acres. T.R. and Sally are both college educated, and Sally is a social services employee. T.R. has tried farming, dairying, and storekeeping but mostly likes to hunt. T.R. always hires neighbors to help him work his tobacco; although hiring neighbors is unnot usual, T.R. and his hastily assembled crew are always harried because T.R.'s tobacco is always late and is among the last to get to market after Christmas. T.R. likes farming less than devising ways to make farm work easier. T.R. designed and built a tomato wagon to make picking tomatoes easier. While his wife and friends worked the tomatoes, T.R. worked on the wagon. When it was finally ready, it failed on the first day's effort because the brakes proved faulty. The people and tomatoes almost fell off the wagon when it went careening down the hill. Neighbors laughed for the next year about the retired wagon and wondered what T.R. would devise next. T.R. tried dairying but, unfortunately, didn't like to milk regularly. At last report, he was running a small store and enjoying the conversations afforded him by his customers. T.R. said that during deer season he was going to close up, and if anybody wanted him, they'd know where to find him.

Although T.R. is the butt of much humor and has little common sense, he is respected and well liked in the community. T.R. and Sally have worked hard in the church, particularly in organizing activities for the children. T.R. was the first person to hire Larry Douthit. Larry was initially ostracized by some residents as a "hippy," but because T.R. opened the door to him, others followed suit. T.R. is an "educated fool" who has "no common sense." He is admired for his generosity, sense of humor, and humility and is respected for his efforts, though they are often misdirected. T.R. is a man of worth.

Worth is assumed until demonstrations of worthlessness prove otherwise. Worth is not easily lost and need not be guarded with excessive diligence. Rather than being a value that must be achieved and perpetually reachieved, worth is assumed until severe transgressions prove its nonexistence.

The most common way of becoming worthless is not to work. One may also become worthless by drinking too much; yet, here again, the distinction depends on work. If a drunkard works hard on a regular basis, he is not necessarily worthless. One man drinks almost every afternoon and continues during most evenings. When drinking, he usually associates with male friends, playing cards or just gossiping in his garage. He works hard during the mornings and afternoons, supports his family, and thus fulfills his economic responsibilities to his children. Furthermore, some people feel that he drinks so much because his wife and her parents disapprove so heartily of his drinking. Because of this, and also because he doesn't cause any trouble when drunk, he is not considered worthless (except by his parents-in-law).

One who is disruptive to community harmony or is a "troublemaker" may also be considered worthless. Lloyd Miller is a self-ordained preacher and a part-time deputy sheriff and considers himself to be guardian of community morality. Lloyd is a meddler. He is quite visible in the community and, because he prowls around in the mountains, is frequently suspected of spying on his neighbors. Lloyd found the marijuana growing in the woods and took the sheriff to it; when the Presnell boy was sent to prison for shooting his friend during a poker game, Lloyd tried unsuccessfully to organize a petition "to get the Presnells thrown off the creek"; Lloyd supposedly stole some money from coworkers when working in the mines; Lloyd shot one of J.B.'s hunting dogs one night; when his tomatoes got the blight, Lloyd is rumored to have walked in his neighbors' tomatoes so that theirs would blight too (one man finally put up a "No Trespassing" sign to try to keep him out); when T.R.'s cows got out because T.R. didn't get around to mending his fences, Lloyd put up a sign reading "All Trespassing Animals Will Be Shot." Lloyd is always seen in the company of his "poor" wife and daughter "so nobody will shoot him"; Lloyd is "not worth shooting, or he'd a been dead already." Lloyd works hard to make a living and supports his family. But, Lloyd seems perpetually to stir up trouble. Lloyd is a troublemaker, a meddler who cannot be trusted; he is "worthless."

A person of worth has the common sense to know when not to interfere, when to leave well enough alone. According to the "high sheriff" (as distinguished from the deputies), "Folks 'round here are the nicest you'd want to meet anywhere. Sometimes trouble gets started, but you can usually avoid problems by using your common sense." The high sheriff is respected for leaving well enough alone much of the time. The highway patrol "boys," however, over whom the county has little control, "don't know when to leave things alone" and, accordingly, are resented.

Demonstrations of worth depend primarily on work. Claude Phillips, who resides with his family at the bottom of the creek, spends much of his waking hours reclining on a couch on the porch. Claude is "only renting"; he is "no kin" to any of the Phillipses in the community and is "on welfare 'cause he's too lazy to work." Claude is worthless and ignored. Thus from an emic point of view, a large category of "worthwhile" people exists in the community, some of whom have had more success at manipulating the environment and the economy than others, and a minuscule group of worthless individuals, who are normally discussed only when outsiders pry into their existence. For most purposes, this small group does not exist. When kinship is queried, they seem to be kin to no one, even though their family names may be the same as those of community members. For residential analysis they are forgotten, and when the question is pursued, they are "only renting." They are temporary residents, not really part of the community. Further probing reveals that "they're on welfare 'cause they're too lazy to work." Thus, although another family may be as poor as the worthless family, if they work, they are included in the large category of "community" because persons of worth work. The poor family of worth will be defended to the outsider, and instances of individual achievement in spite of hardship will be told and retold. This distinction between worthless and worthwhile seems to depend on whether the individual in question makes some effort at coping with subsistence.

"Work" and "public work" have different meanings in rural Appalachia. Public work includes any job that entails working under someone else's authority for a regular salary, normally with no return from the job other than the wage earned and possible fringe benefits. Work in industry, education, or government would thus be included in this category. The broader category of "work" includes any economic activity that contributes to subsistence or maintenance, with the specific exclusion of "public work." Public work most commonly results in wages; work may or may not result in wages. Work thus includes gardening, child rearing, housekeeping, farming, timbering, and mining for personal or private profit and not in industry, and a tremendous variety of other, often daily, activities of this nature. Thus, although I was never asked, "Do you work?" I was frequently asked, "Do you do public work?" the assumption being that I, like most people, work. Thus, when an individual is considered worthless because he won't work, he is being criticized not for not getting a job (that is, a public job) but for not making at least some effort at coping with basic subsistence problems. Furthermore, although public assistance is not a very "worthwhile" source of subsistence, families receiving public assistance are not by that fact alone classed as worthless. Thus, some families are part of the "most folks" category who are in fact receiving assistance in the form of welfare or food stamps, although this is an undesirable alternative.

Worth is not a limited good, nor is it in limited supply,

since every individual has a potentially equal and personal amount.[12] Through the individual's personal decision to act in a worthless manner, he is viewed as lacking worth. Thus the worthlessness of one individual in no way increases the worth of another. In fact, in certain situations such as marriage, an individual's worthlessness may place an unusual and undeserved burden on another, which may, theoretically, cause the latter person to lose worth. Jane Presnell is a hard-working woman who is married to a worthless man. Cicero Presnell is worthless because he stays drunk most of the time and is "too lazy to work." Jane runs her household, takes care of the children, and works for people in the community. Jane is respected for her efforts and is a woman of worth. Theoretically, Jane could give up trying to defy Cicero's behavior and would become worthless too. Likewise, her children could follow in their father's footsteps and become worthless.

Although worth may be lost, it may also be regained through changing behavior. T.R. Campbell went through a worthless period for seveal years after marriage and became a carousing drunk. T.R. had a serious automobile accident and "hasn't touched a drop since." Another "worthless drunk" underwent a religious conversion during a revival in a local church and has since been a hard-working, religious, responsible supporter of his family. Rebecca Phillips's young daughter-in-law is worthless because she "lays around all the time and won't do nothing." Although her parents are worthless " 'cause they're on welfare and Darlene never learned to do nothing," there is a good possibility that Darlene will not stay worthless. Although she is a married woman and therefore a responsible adult, Darlene is only fifteen and, through the help of her affines, will probably learn to do the things that women arc supposed to do.

Community evaluation of work, and thus the worth of an individual, is the major factor in determining integration or social interaction with newcomers. Although initial social interaction is avoided, the newcomer is closely observed. After several weeks, residents are able to determine whether or not the newcomers seem to be working in some way, and they will then initiate interaction. The cultivation of closer personal relationships depends on numerous other factors such as value orientations, personality, and religious philosophy. But in terms of basic acceptance, which in the rural mountain community has a great deal to do with determining a comfortable existence even for those who are not dependent on agriculture, the criterion of work, and thus worth, is foremost.

As defined, worth is assumed to exist in people and is innate intelligence or common sense that motivates rational judgment. Men and women possess worth in the same way, although because of the division of labor by sex, it is manifest in different ways. Community ideas of worth assume an ideal self-sufficiency and independence of the individual, although the individual of worth recognizes the rational limitations of such individualism and the value of cooperative action in specific circumstances. There are only a few worthless individuals in each community. Thus egalitarianism as a conceptual system applies only to community members, the "most folks" category, and excludes the few worthless individuals.

LEVELING MECHANISMS

Several leveling mechanisms operate in the community that both encourage and reaffirm conformity to this ideal of egalitarianism. The first of these is collective history and shared experience. Common origins, shared history, and common environmental difficulties equalize the status and alternatives of residents in the community and reinforce the necessity of cooperation among residents.

The second mechanism that acts to reaffirm equality is communitywide self-denigration, such as that expressed in the phrase "We're all just plain mountain folks." This phrase, or a variant such as "Aw, we're just poor farmers," was often offered as an explanation for behavior in general but was used in particular when praise or compliments were offered concerning some activity or possession. In response to a statement on the soundness of his relatively new brick home, one man replied that "it'll sorta do for old mountain people."

Likewise, in response to a comment on the beauty of the 150-plus acres of land he owned, another man replied, "Rocks; I call it rocks . . . I'm land poor." This attitude of humility is a desire to be inconspicuous.[13] By avoiding status competition based on wealth, the community maintains equality and stability in its relationships.

Consistent with this desire to be inconspicuous is a third mechanism, a code of avoidance of display. This code is most noticeable in the fact that there was, until recently, a lack of formal church weddings in the rural southern Appalachian community. Elopement was the most common means by which couples in the community are married. Normally, a couple would "slip off" to a justice of the peace in a nearby county or occasionally a nearby state to be married. The desire for secrecy may or may not be a factor involved. In one case, the mother of a fourteen-year-old bride went along to witness the ceremony and to give consent for her minor daughter. In another case, the bride's father witnessed the marriage. In other cases, couples slipped off alone or with friends and returned the same or the next day.

Some explained elopement by noting that preachers were not often available for performing such ceremonies in the distant past when the custom originated and that couples slipped off from necessity. Others noted that "folks just always have" or "we didn't want to make no fuss." One college-educated woman did have a church wedding in Rocky Creek during the 1960s. As a deviation from the norm, this ceremony was well remembered and criticized, at least in the early 1970s. Neighbors said that the parents of the bride were simply trying to "show off." The bride's mother, in turn, told of the trauma of the event both for her and for her daughter.

BEING UPPITY

Just as part of the myth of Lincoln is the "antithetical rags-to-riches success story," implicit in the myth of egalitarianism is the potential for deviation from this ideal. Lincoln is thus repesentative of "the American success story, the rags to riches motif, the ideals of the ambitious. As the equal of all men, Lincoln was the representative of the common man, both as his spokesman and his kind; now, as the man who had gone 'from the log cabin to the White House,' he became the superior man, who had not inherited but earned that superior status and thereby proved to everyone that all men could do as he had. Lincoln thereby symbolized the two great collective but antithetical ideals of American democracy" (Warner 1959:272). In this respect egalitarianism and independence become antithetical. Egalitarianism results in a cooperative body of equals, whereas independence results in potential social deviants, those who become superior to the majority, just as Lincoln "had not inherited but earned that superior status and thereby proved to everyone that all men could do as he had." Implicit in both myths is the potential for deviation from the ideal of egalitarianism, the emergence of the individual who is superior to "common folk," who is "uppity." On occasion, the community must deal with this potential deviation. As a consequence, a fourth type of leveling activity functions primarily to chastise or, more realistically, to harass deviants from the egalitarian principle. These leveling activities are gossip, petty theft, and vandalism, which are sanctions perpetuated on members of the community who deviate from the norm by having aspirations for or pretensions of higher class.[14]

Gossip is in perpetual movement along complex and overlapping networks; it is the primary means by which local information is circulated and evaluations are formulated and circulated throughout the community. Gossip provides the medium for expressing personal and collective evaluations of behavior and allows one to avoid face-to-face encounters. Negative sanctions generated along gossip lines remain anonymous and can therefore generate no personal hostilities or confrontations. Sanctions circulate to an individual in the form of "I heard about . . . [your behavior]." Object lessons presented in the framework of gossip provide negative sanctions that indirectly affect behavior; thus, "Did you hear about the awful thing that so-and-so did?" warns the individual of the negative consequences of a particular course of action. Gossip is probably the most significant social-control mechanism operating in the community.

Petty theft and vandalism are a second type of sanction against "uppity" behavior. Petty theft includes theft of such things as chickens and gasoline; that is, items whose loss represents no great financial disaster or incident worthy of widespread publicity or legal recourse; it represents simple harassment. The victims' reactions were consistently controlled irritation and, to some extent, embarrassment.

Vandalism was most often carried out on Halloween night, although isolated incidents might occur here and there throughout the year. One such incident involved the burning of the victim's hay crop in the middle of the road. As far as could be ascertained, the perpetrators of the incidents were teenage boys in the community whose number included close relatives of the victim. The perpetrators of such crimes considered the incidents extremely amusing and stated that they would love to have seen the victim's reaction. One boy complained, "There's been no fun around here since Halloween."

These incidents are considerd leveling mechanisms, rather than simple Halloween jokes or nonmalicious theft, because of the selective nature of the incidents and victims and because of the particular qualities of the individuals who were consistently victimized. The victims of such harassment were persons in the community who had pretensions. The notion of aspirations for a higher class is, in this sense, not necessarily a function of absolute wealth but of attitudes toward the community itself. One victimized individual was a successful, but by no means the wealthiest, member of the community and was, in fact, one of the more poorly educated residents. He exhibited, however, a condescending attitude toward community life and "mountain ways" in favor of his ideal of cosmopolitan lifestyles. For example, this was the man who most frequently apologized for differences between the standard of living in the mountain community and his conception of middle-class society in general, for activities that he considered "low class" and "backward," and for the lack of services in the area that he assumed were available in urban areas.

The community resident can be innovative or financially successful without necessarily inviting criticism. Criticism is incurred primarily by an individual's negative attitude toward community life and neighbors. Thus the husband and wife in one fairly successful family were both college educated, were highly respected and admired for their agricultural orientation, their humility, and their apparently sincere interest in most members of the community, irrespective of their financial status. They had volleyball games and other events in their yard, at which even the young adults from the poorest families in the community felt welcome. Though they were highly respected, no one felt that they considered themselves better than or different from anyone else in the community.

In summary, explanations for the existence and persistence of the myth of egalitarianism lie in the social and economic matrix of the community's past and present. The belief system emerges from the complex of social and economic factors and is reinforced through social and economic alternatives for action or through opportunities available to the individual.

Community integration is reinforced through common roots and shared experience. The individual's worth to the community is measured by the assumption of personal responsibilities, regard for community norms, and modesty about one's own financial status. The individual's disparagement or denial of the way of life in the community poses a threat to networks of community cooperation in reciprocal relationships, whereas equality provides the mechanism for cooperation. Deviations in the form of refusal to put forth any effort at self-preservation, disregard for community norms, or general disruption of community harmony thus threaten community integration as well as the individual's important reciprocal relationships and economic welfare. Gossip, petty theft, and vandalism are effective sanctions that aim to realign individual interaction.

Independence and egalitarianism are cultural ideals, or myths; socioeconomic stratification and dependence are economic realities. The myths of independence and egalitarianism, however, perform necessary integrative functions for members of the community, in the sense that the myths provide the mechanism whereby the common sentiments of rootedness in the land, kinship interrelations, and the value of self-sufficiency achieved through work are symbolically repesented. Two fundamental American symbols of egalitarianism that are highly valued in the community—democratic equality and the importance of the common folk—are thus expressed. The end result of this expression of unity is cooperation in social and economic relationships.

THE UNCERTAIN FUTURE

When Gennifer got to George's store she stopped at the gas pumps for a little gas, realizing that in her rush to get home she had forgotten to fill up at the Pay-Lo in town, where gas was considerably cheaper. As she stepped inside to pay, she chatted briefly with her neighbor Maggie as her three-year-old placed the carefully selected red sucker up on the counter. Gennifer's husband had had a long visit with Maggie earlier in the week, as Maggie had called to talk about a candidate for local office whom she was supporting. As she drove away from the store, Gennifer noticed with some amusement that Maggie had gone only as far as the parking lot and was now engaged in animated conversation with another neighbor and fellow Republican.

During an election or community emergency or when an issue of local public concern is under consideration, George's store becomes a locus for discussion, information exchange, and mobilization of community opinion. On election day, people stop in on their way to and from the polling place to discuss the progress of the election or the voter turnout. Maggie herself stays in the middle of these events. As an elected county official who, through the years, has managed to build a strong power base, Maggie wields a considerable amount of influence and repesents for the local community the full power of the local political party organization.

As a person with considerable access to and understanding of county political and legal processes, Maggie is a highly valued and simultaneously resented intermediary between the individual in the local community—who quite often feels powerless—and the county government. Maggie can assist in problems with traffic violations, local tax assessments, tobacco allotments, or federal income tax returns, and she does so readily, building up obligations from her neighbors, who either feel that they have little means for resolving such problems or can ill afford to take time off work in order to drive all the way into town to solve a problem. While Maggie's skills, knowledge, and influence are highly valued by her neighbors, who know that she is always available to help solve a problem, she is resented. A woman of considerable means, with a caustic tongue, a ready opinion, and a strong will, she will call in the many favors owed come election time. She might also ask the appropriate neighbor for some sort of action on issues of concern to her—to write a letter, sign a petition, support a candidate, or make a telephone call.

As newcomers arrive and take an increasingly active role in the life of the community, differences in values become apparent. During an election, the extent of local political obligations and influence becomes obvious. Maggie has made it a point to know and, on occasion, to cultivate and encourage the participation of some newcomers in local political activities; she has also created obligations to herself among newcomers. However, the extent to which this pattern of local political influence will continue, as more newcomers arrive and identify with each other rather than with local neighbors, remains to be seen. Also, newcomers arrive with their own views and with no obligations to the local political process; while the exchange of favors can tie them into a set of obligations, newcomers are not consistently responsive to these obligations or dependable, since they may have their own, and perhaps different, ideas about community goals, with little recognition or respect for the local patterns of power, obligation, and influence, cultivated over a period of years.

With increasing numbers of newcomers who are making their presence felt, their different points of view known, their different styles of accomplishing tasks evident, and even their diffeent goals for community apparent, comes increasing change in the tenuous fabric of community. As Stephenson has suggested for Shiloh, "There can be little doubt that the newcomers' influence on Shiloh is making it a better community in many respects if we measure community vitality by the degree of locality-based association and mutual problem-solving. If, on the other hand, we were to define the strength of community in terms of shared identity or shared sense of place, the picture of Shiloh is more confusing" (1984:198).

Is there a future for the rural southern Appalachian community? Will those patterns of relationship continue to provide stability, continuity, and predictability in the future?

Old people and younger families alike, espcially those who have made a conscious decision to try to "make a life" in their home community after experiencing lifestyles elsewhere, want life to follow time-tested patterns and want the land to continue to nurture and give sustenance to those who are temporarily its guardians. As the Bible "offers the promise of continuity and stability in a potentially unstable world," (Humphrey 1984:123), so the seasonal passage of life is most satisfying and comprehensible in its predictability and stability.

Yet young people leave—must leave—in order to make their way. While some have always left, fewer stay behind now and few return. For those who can and do stay to marry and raise their families, the old world of community is changing. Family acreage is sold to outsiders who can afford to pay the high market price. Younger families who stay are given or buy only a small plot, enough for a garden and a mobile home that may eventually be replaced by a house. Very few young people are following in their very few farming parents' footsteps; most seek their route to the American dream through increasing public-work opportunities. The older people lament the increase in the number of houses springing up in the community and the breaking up of farms, yet rejoice in the opportunity to assist their own sons or daughters in setting up housekeeping on their family land in a separate dwelling nearby.

The flood of 1977 brought neighbor into immediate helping or sharing relationships with neighbor and confirmed or reaffirmed older ties of community. This emergency, as well as other minor events that continued to occur throughout the year, tested old patterns that proved viable in binding neighbor to neighbor, in binding new neighbors into old networks, and in reaffirming the locus of interaction in the daily visiting at the local store, in the daily telephone conversations of older women to each other, in the Saturday afternoon trading of gossip in someone's garage over an engine needing repair, or in the Sunday morning discussions in Sunday school and after services on the front yard of the church.

In 1984, grief in the death of an older neighbor is borne not only by his widow, his children in the community, their spouses, their children and grandchildren, and his cousins and their families but by the back-to-the-land newcomer as well, whom he assisted in myriad ways in learning the intricacies of getting cattle to market, fixing an old baler, and neighboring. Neighbors behaved as they were expected to behave during the flooding, and the events surrounding their loss of this valued relative and friend. Community as understood and felt offers predictability. While the future is unclear, the historical legacy, the connectedness with land, the continuity of kinship and friendship ties, and the predictability of neighboring offer some hope for stability in a troubled world.

NOTES

INTRODUCTION

1. Use of the term "community" thus reflects a legacy of Tönnies's (1887) "gemeinschaft/gesellschaft" distinction, in which gemeinschaft "rests in the consciousness of belonging together and the affirmation of the condition of mutual dependence which is posed by that affirmation," a concept that "translates easily enough into community" (Nisbet 1966:74); Durkheim's (1893) notion of the collective conscience or shared beliefs that make of a social group a moral community and that help maintain social solidarity; and Weber's (1925) definition of communal, as distinct from associative, relationships, reflecting Tönnies's gemeinschaft/gesellschaft distinction.

2. Partly in reaction to the limits of "structural functional" analysis in dealing with social relationships that are not centered in definable, discrete, and self-perpetuating groups, Barnes (1954) and, following him, Bott (1957), Mitchell (1969), and others developed the concept of social network analysis. Networks link individuals through ties of kinship, economics, religion, or friendship, and may be single- or multistranded, that is, having one or more types of ties or content. Depending on the content of the network, individual actions toward one another are dominated by certain "norms, beliefs, and values" (Mitchell) associated with that content.

3. My use of "community" is further informed by Calhoun's (1980) synthesis of community as both a moral entity and a complex of social relations based on multistranded relations. These relations may be based on familiarity and predictability, economic obligations, and more "diffuse" obligations including kinship and friendship ties. He further discusses such features as density, characteristic of small populations in which "it becomes possible 'for everyone to know everyone else;' " (Calhoun 1980:118) the "moral import" of multiplex (multistranded) relationships; and "systematicity," which "involves the existence of common principles which establish and order social relationships." (1980:120) Thus, for Calhoun, "through bonds and networks of these kinds, social actors are knit together into communities. . . . As social persons, their behavior can involve other social persons, involuntarily, in a stream of actions, either through interpersonal bonds or as members of corporate groups." (1980:120) It is in the sense of

defining proper rules of action and the limits of action and "in that of accumulated esoterica and personal familiarity, that the community is a culturally defined way of life. It holds its members to a set of rules and standards which allows them the intensity of their interaction." (1980:120)

1. THE COMMUNITIES IN CONTEXT

1. This geographical description of Appalachia is based on the work of John C. and Olive Dame Campbell (see Campbell 1921), who, between 1913 and 1919, strove to describe the social life and environment of what they termed "the Southern Highlands." Their work stands today as the classic definition of the southern and central Appalachian region, based on an assessment of cultural patterns and geography.

2. John Stephenson's analysis of Shiloh (1968), another rural community in western North Carolina, provides a useful description of social classes in such a community, of social change in the mountains, and of the ability of older social structures and personal styles to cope with change. Stephenson approaches the community of Shiloh primarily through the family, looking at the different adaptive patterns of the four family types, corresponding roughly to three social levels, that he finds in Shiloh. Stephenson's work provides to date the most appropriate analysis of social class in the rural community in agriculturally-based southern Appalachia.

4. SEX ROLES AND THE LIFE CYCLE

1. Cf. Carmen Diana Deere and Magdalena Leon de Leal's (1981:350) discussion of the technical division of labor within agricultural activities among Andean peasant communities undergoing change as a result of industrialization; men and women use different tools and women are seen as "helping out." The technical division of labor serves to reinforce a woman's subordination.

2. See Beaver, Putzel, and Schlesinger's (1980) discussion of the mobile-home industry in the south, particularly in the mountain south.

3. See Rosaldo's 1974 discussion of the use of the terms "domestic" and "public," and her 1980 discussion of the limitations and constraints in the use of these terms. Rosaldo (1974) suggests a universal distinction between public and domestic spheres of life: the domestic sphere, growing from the relationship between mother and infant, "refers to those minimal institutions and modes of activity that are organized immediately around one or more mothers and their children;" the public sphere stems from the freeing or perhaps exclusion of men, through a pragmatic division of tasks, from the commitment to infants, and refers to "activities, institutions, and forms of association that link, rank, and organize, or subsume particular mother-child (domestic) groups" (1974:23).

4. Cf. Deere and de Leal's (1981) discussion of industrialization and the sexual division of labor in the Andes. "As men become increasingly proletarianized, women take up the household's secondary activity, subsistence

agricultural production, almost as an extension of domestic world."
(1981:188).
    5. Cf. Collins and Finn (1976).
    6. For a summary of the implications of women's widespread movement
into low-wage production with the introduction of capitalist modes of production and the resulting subordination of women with capitalism, see the
special issue of *Signs* entitled *Development and the Sexual Division of Labor*
(vol. 7, no. 2, winter 1981). In that volume, Leacock quoted the United
Nations Division for Economic and Social Information, Department of Public Information bulletin "Worsening Situation of Women Will Be Main Issue
Confronting Commission on the Status of Women" as follows: "A 'review of
progress . . . made on the basis of information provided by 86 governments'
. . . showed that 'in most countries the situation of women from the so-called
"backward sectors" of the population had worsened . . . in particular with
respect to employment and education for women in rural areas and in the so-
called marginal urban sectors.' . . . Women in developing countries were
increasingly being used as a cheap source of labor" (1981:475-76).

6. COMMUNITY: PAST, PRESENT, AND FUTURE

    1. Portions of the following discussion have been published as Beaver
1978.
    2. Cf. W.L. Warner's (1959) discussion of "integrating" and "individ-
uating" social institutions in Yankee City; the "symbolic life of Americans"
as expressed primarily through public ritual; and the selective nature of the
recognition of historical "facts."
    3. Cf. Bronislaw Malinowski 1948 for a discussion of myth as validating
and reinforcing the order of social reality and of social relationships and as
providing a social "charter" for the organization of relationships. Mary
Douglas (1967:52) notes with respect to the "relation of myth to social
reality" that "the ideal is not attainable." S.F. Nadel (1942) discusses the
importance of the "mythic charter" of the Nupe kingdom as a background
for cultural "commonness" and political unity.
    4. Many works dealing with specific areas within the Appalachian re-
gion generalize the region where history is concerned; for example, Caudill
1963.
    5. See also Gazaway 1969 and Fetterman 1970 for thoughtful analyses of
two specific communities. These analyses are nevertheless based on this
assumption.
    6. See Lewis 1970 and Lewis, Johnson, Askins 1978 for important dis-
cussion of Appalachia as "colony."
    7. Cf. Whisnant 1973.
    8. One old man did say that, since his grandson had visited Germany and
had come across some folk there with his same last name, he guessed his
family "come from Germany and was Jews."
    9. Cf. Brown 1950, 1952; Pearsall 1959; Coles 1971; Schwarzweller,
Brown, and Mangalam 1971; and Beaver 1976.

10. "Worth" as used in this context is in some ways, comparable to Mediterranean notions of "honor" as described by J.K. Campbell (1964), Pitt-Rivers (1968), and Persistiany (1966) and of "brains" as described by Friedl (1962). With respect to the latter concept, Friedl writes: "The villagers assume that intelligence and self-control are basic human qualities which differentiate men from animals. The villagers are in many ways committed humanists and assume that once these traits are developed each man will have the strength to face life and its vasana (trials and pains)" (1962:77). "Worth" is likewise comparable to "honor" in the sense that it refers to "a sign of the recognition of the excellence or worth of a person . . . [and] expresses the worth, whether this is an economic value in a market, or social worth evaluated in a complex of competing groups and individuals" (Campbell 1964:268).

11. According to Cratis Williams, this graphic and poetic phrase was a favorite of his father's.

12. Greek honor has, according to Campbell's qualification, features of a "Limited Good" in the sense that Foster describes certain qualities that "exist in finite quantity and are always in short supply" (Foster 1965:296).

13. Cf. certain mechanisms described by Foster by which "essential stability" is maintained in peasant cultures. Foster describes "self-correcting mechanisms that guard the community balance" of a particular "good" or "desired thing," and thus of the "status quo in relationships." That is, at the level of the individual or family, one rule of behavior is "Do not reveal evidence of material or other improvements in your relative position, lest you invite sanctions; should you display improvement, take action necessary to neutralize the consequences" (1965:303). Also, "accounts of peasant communities stress that in traditional villages people do not compete for prestige with material symbols such as dress, housing, or food, nor do they compete for authority by seeking leadership roles. In peasant villages one notes a strong desire to look and act like everyone else, to be inconspicuous in position and behavior" (1965:303).

14. These activities may be compared to the second of three "self-correcting mechanisms that guard the community balance" described by Foster. This mechanism is "Informal, Unorganized Group Action" described as follows: "The ideal man strives for moderation and quality in his behavior. Should he attempt to better his comparative standing, thereby threatening village stability, the informal and usually unorganized sanctions appear. This is the 'club,' and it takes the form of gossip, slander, backbiting, character assassination, witchcraft or the threat of witchcraft, and sometimes actual physical aggression. These negative sanctions usually represent no formal community decisions, but they are at least as effective as if authorized by law. Concern with public opinion is one of the most striking characteristics of peasant communities" (Foster 1965:305).

BIBLIOGRAPHY

Appalachian Land Ownership Task Force. 1983. *Who Owns Appalachia? Landownership and Its Impact.* Lexington: Univ. Press of Kentucky.

Arthur, John P. 1915. *A History of Watauga County, North Carolina.* Richmond: Everett Waddey.

Arthur, John Preston. 1973. *Western North Carolina: A History, 1730-1913.* Spartanburg, S.C.: Reprint.

Barnes, J.A. 1954. Class and Communities in a Norwegian Island Parish. *Human Relations* 7(1):39-58.

Beaver, Patricia D. 1976. Symbols and Social Organization in an Appalachian Mountain Community. Ph.D. diss., Duke University.

_____. 1978. Independence, Egalitarianism, and the Historical Myth. *Appalachian Journal* 5(4):400-411.

_____. 1984. Appalachian Cultural Adaptations: An Overview. In *Cultural Adaptation to Mountain Environments,* ed. Patricia Beaver and Burton Purrington, pp. 73-93. Southern Anthropological Society Proceedings no. 17. Athens: Univ. of Georgia Press.

Beaver, Patricia D., Mary Jane Putzel, and Tom Schlesinger. 1980. Trailers: The Factory, the Business, the Owners. *Southern Exposure* 8(1):14-25.

Billings, Dwight. 1982. Appalachian Studies: Class, Culture, and Politics, I. *Appalachian Journal* 9:134-40.

Blackmun, Ora. 1977. *Western North Carolina: Its Mountains and Its People to 1880.* Boone, N.C.: Appalachian Consortium Press.

Bott, Elizabeth. 1957. *Family and Social Network.* London: Tavistock Publications.

Brown, James S. 1950. The Social Organization of an Isolated Kentucky Mountain Neighborhood. Ph.D. diss., Harvard University.

_____. 1952. The Conjugal Family and the Extended Family Group. *American Sociological Review* 17:297-306.

Brown, James S., and George A. Hillery, Jr. 1962. The Great Migration, 1940-1960. In *The Southern Appalachian Region*, ed. Thomas R. Ford, pp. 34-78. Lexington: Univ. of Kentucky Press.

Brown, James S., Harry Schwarzweller, and Joseph J. Mangalam. 1963. Kentucky Mountain Migration and the Stem Family: An American Variation on a Theme by Le Play. *Rural Sociology* 28:48-69.

Calhoun, C.J. 1980. Community: Toward a Variable Conceptualization for Comparative Research. *Social History* 5(1):105-29.

Campbell, J.K. 1964. *Honour, Family, and Patronage.* Oxford: Clarendon Press.

Campbell, John C., 1969. *The Southern Highlander and His Homeland.* Lexington: Univ. Press of Kentucky. Orig. pub. New York: Sage Foundation, 1921.

Caudill, Harry. 1963. *Night Comes to the Cumberlands.* Boston: Little, Brown and Company.

_____. 1972. Appalachia. In *Who Owns the Land? A Primer on Land Reform in the United States*, ed. Peter Barnes and Larry Casalino, p. 33. Berkeley, Calif.: Center for Rural Studies.

_____. 1973. *My Land Is Dying.* New York: Dutton.

_____. 1976. *A Darkness at Dawn.* Lexington: Univ. Press of Kentucky.

_____. 1982. Personal communication.

Center for Improving Mountain Living. 1984. County Development Information for Ashe County. Cullowhee, N.C.

_____. 1984. County Development Information for Watauga County. Cullowhee, N.C.

Coles, Robert. 1971. Migrants, Sharecroppers, Mountaineers. Volume II of Children of Crisis. Little, Brown & Company: Boston.

Collins, Thomas W., and Clata L. Finn. 1976. Mountain Women in a Changing Labor Market. *Tennessee Anthropologist* 1(2):104-11.

Deere, Carmen Diana and Magdalena Leon de Leal. 1981. Peasant Production, Proletarianization, and the Sexual Division of Labor. *Signs* 7(2):338-360.

Deyton, Jason B. 1947. The Toe River Valley to 1865. *North Carolina Historical Review* 24:423-66.

Douglas, Mary. 1967. The Meaning of Myth, with Special Reference to "La Geste d'Asdiwal." In *The Structural Study of Myth and Totemism*, ed. Edmund Leach, pp. 49-70. London: Tavistock Publications.

Durkheim, Emile. 1893. *The Division of Labor in Society.* Trans. George Simpson. New York: Free Press, 1964.

Duvall, John A. 1984. A View of Ashe County in the Twentieth Century. In *The Heritage of Ashe County,* vol. 1, pp. 27-30. Winston-Salem, N.C.: Ashe County Heritage Book Committee in cooperation with the History Division of Hunter Publishing Company.

Efird, Cathy. 1980. Land Ownership and Property Taxation in North Carolina. In *Appalachian Land Ownership Study. Vol. 4: North Carolina,* pp. 1-46. Appalachian Land Ownership Task Force. Boone, N.C.: Center for Appalachian Studies.

Eller, Ronald. 1978. Industrialization and Social Change in Appalachia, 1880-1930. In *Colonialism in Modern America,* ed. Helen Lewis, Linda Johnson, and Donald Askins, pp. 35-46. Boone, N.C.: Appalachian Consortium Press.

————. 1979. Land and Family: An Historical View of Preindustrial Appalachia. *Appalachian Journal* 6:83-110.

————. 1982. *Miners, Millhands, and Mountaineers: Industrialization of the Appalachian South, 1880-1930.* Knoxville: Univ. of Tennessee Press.

Estabrook, Arthur. 1926. Presidential Address: Blood Seeks Environment. *Eugenical News* 11:106-14.

Fetterman, John. 1970. *Stinking Creek.* New York: Dutton.

Fisher, Stephen L., and Mary Harnish. 1981. Losing a Bit of Ourselves: The Decline of the Small Farmer. In *Appalachia/America: Proceedings of the 1980 Appalachian Studies Conference,* ed. Wilson Somerville, pp. 68-88. Boone, N.C.: Appalachian Consortium Press; Johnson City, Tenn. East Tennessee State University.

Fiske, John. 1897. *Old Virginia and Her Neighbors.* Boston: Houghton, Mifflin.

Fletcher, Arthur. 1963. *Ashe County: A History* Jefferson, N.C.: Ashe County Research Assoc.

Ford, Henry Jones. 1966. *The Scotch-Irish in America.* Hamden, Conn.: Archon Books.

Foster, John M. 1965. Peasant Society and the Image of the Limited Good. *American Anthropologist* 67:293-315.

French, Lawrence, and Jim Hornbuckle, eds. 1981. *The Cherokee Perspective.* Boone, N.C.: Appalachian Consortium Press.

Friedl, Ernestine. 1962. *Vasilika: A Village in Modern Greece.* New York: Holt, Rinehart and Winston.

Frost, William Goodell. 1899. Our Contemporary Ancestors in the Southern Mountains. *Atlantic Monthly* 83:311-19.

Gaventa, John. 1980. *Power and Powerlessness: Quiescence and Rebellion in an Appalachian Valley.* Urbana: Univ. of Illinois Press.

Gazaway, Rena. 1969. *The Longest Mile.* Garden City: Doubleday.

Goodman, A.D. et al. 1977. *Rambling through Ashe.* Ashe County, N.C.: Bicentennial Historical Committee.

Green, Archie. 1971. *Only a Miner.* Urbana: Univ. of Illinois Press.

Hirsch, Nathaniel D.M. 1928. An Experimental Study of the East Kentucky Mountaineers. *Genetic Psychology Monographs* 3:183-244.

Holbrook, B. Beatrice. 1984. Ironworks in Ashe and Alleghany Counties. In *The Heritage of Ashe County,* vol. 1, pp. 15-16. Winston-Salem, N.C.: Ashe County Heritage Book Committee in cooperation with the History Division of Hunter Publishing Company.

Humphrey, Richard. 1984. Religion and Place in Southern Appalachia. In *Cultural Adaptation to Mountain Environments.* ed. Patricia Beaver and Burton Purrington, pp. 122-41. Southern Anthropological Society Proceedings no. 17. Athens: Univ. of Georgia Press.

Jones, Loyal. 1977. Old-Time Baptists and Mainline Christianity. In *An Appalachian Symposium,* ed. J.W. Williamson, pp. 120-30. Boone, N.C.: Appalachian State Univ. Press.

Kephart, Horace. 1976. *Our Southern Highlanders.* Knoxville: Univ. of Tennessee Press. Orig. pub. New York: Outing Publishing, 1913.

Langley, Joan, and Wright Langley. 1975. *Yesterday's Asheville.* Miami: Seamen.

Leacock, Eleanor. 1981. History, Development, and the Division of Labor by Sex: Implications for Organization. *Signs* 7(2):474-91.

League of Women Voters of Watauga County, N.C. 1984. *Watauga County Handbook.* Boone, N.C.: Minor's Printing.

Lewis, Helen. 1970. Fatalism or the Coal Industry? *Mountain Life and Work* 46(11):4-15.

———. 1981. Film History of Appalachia. Film Project Proposal from Appalshop Film Studios submitted to Committee for Public Broadcasting/Annenberg School of Communications.

Lewis, Helen, and Edward Knipe. 1970. The Colonialism Model: The Apalachian Case. In Lewis, Johnson, and Askins 1978:9-31.

———. Lewis, Helen, Linda Johnson, and Donald Askins, eds. 1978.

INDEX

Colonialism in Modern America: The Appalachian Case. Boone, N.C.: Appalachian Consortium Press.

Leyburn, James Graham. 1962. *The Scotch Irish: A Social History.* Chapel Hill: Univ. of North Carolina Press.

Maggard, Sally. 1981. From Farmers to Miners: The Decline of Agriculture in Eastern Kentucky. In *Science and Agricultural Developments,* ed. Lawrence Busch, pp. 25-66. Totowa, N.J.: Alanheld, Osmun.

Malinowski, Bronislaw. 1948. *Magic, Science, and Religion.* Boston: Beacon Press.

McKesson, Charles F. 1984. Sutherland. *The Heritage of Ashe County,* vol. 1, pp. 54-55. Winston-Salem, N.C.: Ashe County Heritage Book Committee in cooperation with the History Division of Hunter Publishing Company.

Miles, Emma Bell. 1975. *The Spirit of the Mountains.* Knoxville: Univ. of Tennessee Press. Orig. pub. New York-Pott, 1905.

Mitchell, J. Clyde, 1969. The Concept and Use of Social Networks. In *Social Networks in Urban Situations,* ed. J. Clyde Mitchell, pp. 1-50. Manchester: Manchester Univ. Press.

Moretz, Ray. n.d. Self-Sufficiency in a Mountain Community. Unpublished manuscript.

————. 1979. The Impact of Recreational Development on Agriculture in Watauga County. In *Citizen Participation in Rural Land Use Planning for the Tennessee Valley,* ed. Lindsay Jones, pp. 56-61. Nashville: Agricultural Marketing Project.

————. 1980. Watauga County, North Carolina: A Case Study on Land. In *Appalachian Land Ownership Study. Vol. 4: North Carolina,* pp. 98-160. Appalachian Land Ownership Task Force. Boone, N.C.: Center for Appalachian Studies.

Nadel, S.F. 1942. *A Black Byzantium.* London: Oxford Univ. Press.

Nisbet, Robert A. 1966. *The Sociological Tradition.* New York: Basic Books.

Owsley, Frank Lawrence. 1949. *Plain Folk of the Old South.* Baton Rouge: Louisiana State Univ. Press. Reprinted Chicago: Quadrangle, 1965.

Parker, Delmas. 1975. The Development of Black Education in Ashe County, 1870-1964. Unpublished manuscript.

Parton, Mary F., ed. 1925. *The Autobiography of Mother Jones.* Chicago: Kerr.

Pearsall, Marion. 1959. *Little Smoky Ridge.* Tuscaloosa: Univ. of Alabama Press.

Perdue, Theda. 1979. *Slavery and the Evolution of Cherokee Society,*
    1540-1866. Knoxville: Univ. of Tennessee Press.
Peristiany, J.G. 1966. *Honour and Shame.* Chicago: Univ. of Chicago
    Press.
Pitt-Rivers, Julian. 1968. Honor. In *International Encyclopedia of*
    the Social Sciences, ed. David L. Sills, vol. 6, pp. 503-11. New
    York: Macmillan and The Free Press.
Price, Overton W., 1901. Practical Forestry in the Southern Appala-
    chians. In *Yearbook of the Department of Agriculture: 1900,* pp.
    357-69. Washington: Government Printing Office.
Proctor, Roy E., and T. Kelley White. 1967. Agriculture: A Reassess-
    ment. In *The Southern Appalachian Region: A Survey,* ed.
    Thomas R. Ford, pp. 87-101. Lexington: Univ. of Kentucky Press.
Proffitt, Robert C. 1984. Plum Tree Township. In *The Heritage of*
    Watauga County. pp. 60-62. The Genealogical Society of Watauga
    County. Winston-Salem, N.C.: Hunter Publishing.
Raitz, Karl B., and Richard Ulack. 1984. *Appalachia: A Regional*
    Geography. Boulder: Westview Press.
Ralph, Julian. 1903. Our Appalachian Americans. *Harpers Monthly*
    Magazine 107:32-41.
Reck, Gregory G. 1983. Narrative Anthropology. *Anthropology and*
    Humanism Quarterly 8(1):8-12.
Reid, Herbert G. 1982. Appalachian Studies: Class, Culture, and
    Politics, II. *Appalachian Journal* 9:141-48.
Rosaldo, Michelle Z. 1974. Women, Culture, and Society: A Theo-
    retical Overview. In *Women, Culture, and Society,* ed. M.Z.
    Rosaldo and Louise Lamphere, pp. 17-42. Stanford: Stanford Univ.
    Press.
————. 1980. The Use and Abuse of Anthropology. *Signs*
    5(3):389-417.
Schwarzweller, Harry K., James S. Brown, and J.J. Mangalam. 1971.
    Mountain Families in Transition. University Park: Pennsylvania
    State Univ. Press.
Semple, Ellen Churchill, 1901. The Anglo-Saxons of the Kentucky
    Mountains: A Study in Anthropogeography. *Bulletin of the Amer-*
    ican Geographical Society 42:561-94.
Shapiro, Henry P. 1978. *Appalachia on Our Mind.* Chapel Hill: Univ.
    of North Carolina Press.
Shepperd, M.E. 1935. *Cabins in the Laurel.* Chapel Hill: Univ. of
    North Carolina Press.
Smith, J. Russell. 1916. Farming in Appalachia. *American Review of*
    Reviews 53:329-36.

Snyder, Bob. 1982. Image and Identity in Appalachia. *Appalachian Journal* 9:124-33.

Stephenson, John B. 1968. *Shiloh: A Mountain Community.* Lexington: Univ. of Kentucky Press.

_____. 1984. Escape to the Periphery: Commodifying Place in Rural Appalachia. *Appalachian Journal* 11:187-200.

Tönnies, Ferdinand. 1887. *Gemeinschaft und Gesellschaft.* Trans. by C.P. Loomis, under the title *Fundamental Concepts of Sociology.* New York: American Book, 1940.

Toynbee, Arnold. 1948. *A Study of History*, vol. 2. London: Oxford Univ. Press.

Van Noppen, Ina W., and John J. Van Noppen, 1973. *Western North Carolina since the Civil War.* Boone, N.C.: Appalachian Consortium Press.

Vincent, George. 1898. A Retarded Frontier. *American Journal of Sociology* 4:1-20.

Warner, W. Lloyd. 1959. *The Living and the Dead: A Study of the Symbolic Life of Americans,* vol. 5 New Haven: Yale Univ. Press.

Weber, Max. 1925. *The Theory of Social and Economic Organization.* Trans. A.M. Henderson and T. Parsons. New York: Free Press, 1964.

Weller, Jack. 1965. *Yesterday's People.* Lexington: Univ. Press of Kentucky.

West, Don, n.d. People's Cultural Heritage in Appalachia. Huntington, W.V.: Appalachian Movement Press.

Whisnant, David E. 1973. The Folk Hero in Appalachian Struggle History. *New South* 28(4):30-47.

_____. 1982. Second Level Appalachian History: Another Look at Some Fotched-on Women. *Appalachian Journal* 9:115-23.

Wilhelm, Gene. 1977. Appalachian Isolation. In *An Appalachian Symposium*, ed. J.W. Williamson, pp. 77-91. Boone, N.C.: Appalachian State Univ. Press.

_____. 1978. Folk Settlements in the Blue Ridge. *Appalachian Journal* 5:204-45.

Wilson, James. 1902. Message from the President of the United States transmitting a report of the Secretary of Agriculture in relation to the forests, rivers, and mountains of the southern Appalachian region. Washington, D.C.: Government Printing Office.

Colonialism in Modern America: The Appalachian Case. Boone, N.C.: Appalachian Consortium Press.

Leyburn, James Graham. 1962. *The Scotch-Irish: A Social History.* Chapel Hill: Univ. of North Carolina Press.

Maggard, Sally. 1981. From Farmers to Miners: The Decline of Agriculture in Eastern Kentucky. In *Science and Agricultural Developments,* ed. Lawrence Busch, pp. 25-66. Totowa, N.J.: Alanheld, Osmun.

Malinowski, Bronislaw. 1948. *Magic, Science, and Religion.* Boston: Beacon Press.

McKesson, Charles F. 1984. Sutherland. *The Heritage of Ashe County,* vol. 1, pp. 54-55. Winston-Salem, N.C.: Ashe County Heritage Book Committee in cooperation with the History Division of Hunter Publishing Company.

Miles, Emma Bell. 1975. *The Spirit of the Mountains.* Knoxville: Univ. of Tennessee Press. Orig. pub. New York-Pott, 1905.

Mitchell, J. Clyde, 1969. The Concept and Use of Social Networks. In *Social Networks in Urban Situations,* ed. J. Clyde Mitchell, pp. 1-50. Manchester: Manchester Univ. Press.

Moretz, Ray. n.d. Self-Sufficiency in a Mountain Community. Unpublished manuscript.

———. 1979. The Impact of Recreational Development on Agriculture in Watauga County. In *Citizen Participation in Rural Land Use Planning for the Tennessee Valley,* ed. Lindsay Jones, pp. 56-61. Nashville: Agricultural Marketing Project.

——— 1980. Watauga County, North Carolina: A Case Study on Land. In *Appalachian Land Ownership Study. Vol. 4: North Carolina,* pp. 98-160. Appalachian Land Ownership Task Force. Boone, N.C.: Center for Appalachian Studies.

Nadel, S.F. 1942. *A Black Byzantium.* London: Oxford Univ. Press.

Nisbet, Robert A. 1966. *The Sociological Tradition.* New York: Basic Books.

Owsley, Frank Lawrence. 1949. *Plain Folk of the Old South.* Baton Rouge: Louisiana State Univ. Press. Reprinted Chicago: Quadrangle, 1965.

Parker, Delmas. 1975. The Development of Black Education in Ashe County, 1870-1964. Unpublished manuscript.

Parton, Mary F., ed. 1925. *The Autobiography of Mother Jones.* Chicago: Kerr.

Pearsall, Marion. 1959. *Little Smoky Ridge.* Tuscaloosa: Univ. of Alabama Press.

Perdue, Theda. 1979. *Slavery and the Evolution of Cherokee Society, 1540-1866.* Knoxville: Univ. of Tennessee Press.

Peristiany, J.G. 1966. *Honour and Shame.* Chicago: Univ. of Chicago Press.

Pitt-Rivers, Julian. 1968. Honor. In *International Encyclopedia of the Social Sciences,* ed. David L. Sills, vol. 6, pp. 503-11. New York: Macmillan and The Free Press.

Price, Overton W., 1901. Practical Forestry in the Southern Appalachians. In *Yearbook of the Department of Agriculture: 1900,* pp. 357-69. Washington: Government Printing Office.

Proctor, Roy E., and T. Kelley White. 1967. Agriculture: A Reassessment. In *The Southern Appalachian Region: A Survey,* ed. Thomas R. Ford, pp. 87-101. Lexington: Univ. of Kentucky Press.

Proffitt, Robert C. 1984. Plum Tree Township. In *The Heritage of Watauga County.* pp. 60-62. The Genealogical Society of Watauga County. Winston-Salem, N.C.: Hunter Publishing.

Raitz, Karl B., and Richard Ulack. 1984. *Appalachia: A Regional Geography.* Boulder: Westview Press.

Ralph, Julian. 1903. Our Appalachian Americans. *Harpers Monthly Magazine* 107:32-41.

Reck, Gregory G. 1983. Narrative Anthropology. *Anthropology and Humanism Quarterly* 8(1):8-12.

Reid, Herbert G. 1982. Appalachian Studies: Class, Culture, and Politics, II. *Appalachian Journal* 9:141-48.

Rosaldo, Michelle Z. 1974. Women, Culture, and Society: A Theoretical Overview. In *Women, Culture, and Society,* ed. M.Z. Rosaldo and Louise Lamphere, pp. 17-42. Stanford: Stanford Univ. Press.

———. 1980. The Use and Abuse of Anthropology. *Signs* 5(3):389-417.

Schwarzweller, Harry K., James S. Brown, and J.J. Mangalam. 1971. *Mountain Families in Transition.* University Park: Pennsylvania State Univ. Press.

Semple, Ellen Churchill, 1901. The Anglo-Saxons of the Kentucky Mountains: A Study in Anthropogeography. *Bulletin of the American Geographical Society* 42:561-94.

Shapiro, Henry P. 1978. *Appalachia on Our Mind.* Chapel Hill: Univ. of North Carolina Press.

Shepperd, M.E. 1935. *Cabins in the Laurel.* Chapel Hill: Univ. of North Carolina Press.

Smith, J. Russell. 1916. Farming in Appalachia. *American Review of Reviews* 53:329-36.

Snyder, Bob. 1982. Image and Identity in Appalachia. *Appalachian Journal* 9:124-33.

Stephenson, John B. 1968. *Shiloh: A Mountain Community.* Lexington: Univ. of Kentucky Press.

_____. 1984. Escape to the Periphery: Commodifying Place in Rural Appalachia. *Appalachian Journal* 11:187-200.

Tönnies, Ferdinand. 1887. *Gemeinschaft und Gesellschaft.* Trans. by C.P. Loomis, under the title *Fundamental Concepts of Sociology.* New York: American Book, 1940.

Toynbee, Arnold. 1948. *A Study of History,* vol. 2. London: Oxford Univ. Press.

Van Noppen, Ina W., and John J. Van Noppen, 1973. *Western North Carolina since the Civil War.* Boone, N.C.: Appalachian Consortium Press.

Vincent, George. 1898. A Retarded Frontier. *American Journal of Sociology* 4:1-20.

Warner, W. Lloyd. 1959. *The Living and the Dead: A Study of the Symbolic Life of Americans,* vol. 5 New Haven: Yale Univ. Press.

Weber, Max. 1925. *The Theory of Social and Economic Organization.* Trans. A.M. Henderson and T. Parsons. New York: Free Press, 1964.

Weller, Jack. 1965. *Yesterday's People.* Lexington: Univ. Press of Kentucky.

West, Don, n.d. People's Cultural Heritage in Appalachia. Huntington, W.V.: Appalachian Movement Press.

Whisnant, David E. 1973. The Folk Hero in Appalachian Struggle History. *New South* 28(4):30-47.

_____. 1982. Second Level Appalachian History: Another Look at Some Fotched-on Women. *Appalachian Journal* 9:115-23.

Wilhelm, Gene. 1977. Appalachian Isolation. In *An Appalachian Symposium,* ed. J.W. Williamson, pp. 77-91. Boone, N.C.: Appalachian State Univ. Press.

_____. 1978. Folk Settlements in the Blue Ridge. *Appalachian Journal* 5:204-45.

Wilson, James. 1902. Message from the President of the United States transmitting a report of the Secretary of Agriculture in relation to the forests, rivers, and mountains of the southern Appalachian region. Washington, D.C.: Government Printing Office.

INDEX